COLLABORATIVE LEADERSHIP

Lessons from the Street to the Boardroom

George O'Meara

A $6-billion proven sales leader

For information about permission to reproduce selections from this book,
write to Permissions, BumbleBee Publishing, 3825 Hopyard Road Suite 225,
Pleasanton, CA 94566

For information about special discounts for bulk purchases,
please contact BumbleBee Publishing at ellen@bumblebeemarketing.net

Library of Congress Control Number 2013911216

O'Meara, George.
Collaborative Leadership: Lessons from the Street to the Boardroom
George O'Meara - 1st ed.

ISBN 978-0-9895692-0-0

1. Leadership. 2. Sales. 3. Management.

While the author has made every effort to provide accurate telephone
numbers and Internet addresses at the time of publication, neither the
publisher nor the author assumes any responsibility for errors, or for changes
that occur after publication. Further, the publisher does not have any
control over and does not assume any responsibility for author or
third-party websites or their content.

www.gomeara.com

BumbleBee Publishing
3825 Hopyard Road Suite 225
Pleasanton, CA 94566

Front back cover by Achille Photo
15132 Bel Estos Drive
San Jose, CA 95124
achille@achillephoto.com

Dedicated to my dad, William B. O'Meara, who shared his many insights and reflections and inspired me to be the best I could, every day and in every way. He taught me "life is one big sales call," and I have been striving to make it a good one.

Thank you Dad.

TABLE OF CONTENTS

INTRODUCTION

THE LEADERSHIP GAP

Businesses everywhere are facing a myriad of challenges from shrinking margins to increasing regulation to rapidly evolving technologies. Information is more accessible, products are more commoditized and competitors are less distinctive. Doing business is getting more and more complex—as my dad would say, "Kid, the future ain't what it used to be." Some say these are unprecedented times, and while I agree times are tough, I don't think it's because of the reasons outlined above. I think the biggest challenge businesses face today is a leadership challenge. We can label this challenge with something as dire as the death of leadership or something as simple as a leadership gap. Either way, it is real and it is having real effects on businesses everywhere.

My intention in writing this book is to share what I have learned about leadership on my journey through the information technology industry as an individual contributor in sales for a start-up company, then as a sales manager for a mid-sized hardware company and finally as a senior sales leader for Cisco. My experiences gave me valuable, hard-earned insights that not only transformed how I lead an organization but how I lead my life. I want to share these lessons and insights to help you on your own journey to becoming a better, more effective leader.

I am a salesperson by trade and a leader by calling. In my world, the parallels between the principles of sales and the principles of leadership have made themselves more than obvious, and so have the parallels between leadership and life. A friend asked me if the book was about sales, leadership, transformation or life. I answered, "Yes." As my father used to tell me, "Kid, life is one big sales call." The clincher is that leadership transformation is as pertinent in your personal life as it is in business. Leadership transformation starts from inside a leader and permeates an organization or even family, yielding truly positive results in good times or in bad, in the workplace or in the home.

But this book is about more than creating transformation through leadership. It's about creating transformation through collaboration, an approach I call Collaborative Transformation. The book is also more than a hypothesis; it is theory put into practice and proven in the workplace. After all, at the time I am writing this I am neither an experienced consultant nor a university professor, but a real practitioner who grew an $800-million business into a $6-billion business.

I will tell my story and the lessons I learned through the lens of my life experiences and my career in sales. I will do this for two reasons: One, it makes for a more interesting read. Storytelling is an art that has been with us for ages, and for good reason. Storytelling helps convey information in interesting ways, packaged in the common wrapping of real life experiences we can all relate to in one way or another. Second, I use stories to help convey my ideas because that's how they unfolded for me—in the everyday flow of regular transactions and activities. I'd like to believe that the same things that surprised me in those moments might also surprise you. I'd like to believe that embedded in these stories, behind or underneath the overt lessons I will highlight are subtle nuances that may offer additional insights to many of you.

Who is the intended reader of this book? The readers I had in mind when I first considered writing this book were sales leaders. More specifically, sales leaders who wanted to make a difference in their organizations. One of the questions I love to ask during an interview is, "Let's say you're with this company 10 to 15 years. The day finally comes when you are ready to retire or jog off into the sunset. When you look back, what legacy do you want to have left behind?" This book is for leaders who want to leave a legacy of reshaping a company, of transforming an organization and moving it to a better place through bold leadership, but don't know where to start. This book is also for leaders who have lost their way in the jungle of short-term tactics or who are steeped in the mire of command-and-control cultures. My message to these readers is: There is a way out.

I had multiple inspirations for this book: coaches and mentors, managers and leaders, colleagues and friends, parents and family. I was also inspired by a piece of literature, a watershed of a story in the annals of business literature, a story not only acted out on stages across the world but in the hallways, conference rooms and offices of companies everywhere. I speak, of course, of Arthur Miller's *Death of a Salesman*.

DEATH OF A SALESMAN

Death of a Salesman is a metaphor about all the grand things in life and it's also about the most mundane aspects of day-to-day existence. It's about allowing your work to define who you are. It's also about a changing era and the human condition. For me, this play reflects so much of what we see in business today, from shifting sales models to outmoded styles of leadership to a stubborn resistance to leadership transformation.

Death of a Salesman recounts the tragic tale of Willy Loman. Willy is a 34-year veteran salesman for the Wagner Company in the New England region. He works his route from the trunk of his car, traveling from account to account. His role model is Dave Singleman who reputedly worked his accounts from the phone in a hotel. When Dave died, people from all over attended the funeral. For Willy, that is the epitome of success—to have fame built solely on reputation, to have died the death of a salesman.

Willy's sales are declining. Newer, younger salespeople are climbing the ranks. His time as a traveling salesman is nearing an end. His driving is becoming erratic, a major issue since he is on the road so much, and there are indications that he is contemplating suicide. In a much-quoted scene, Willy goes to his boss and asks for a position in New York. Despite his appeal, Willy is fired. He retorts with a sentiment that resonates all too well in today's economic climate: "I put thirty-four years into this firm, Howard, and now I can't pay my insurance!

You can't eat the orange and throw the peel away—a man is not a piece of fruit!" The play then continues to its bitter conclusion.

What catches my imagination about *Death of a Salesman* isn't the commentary about the human condition. Instead, it's the concept of the death, not of a literal salesman but of a business model. Since 1949, when this play was written, the world has witnessed the metaphorical death of countless Willy Lomans. Some have become outmoded by their own doing, or lack of doing, and some have been superseded by the actions of others or the passage of time. Most tragic of all, some are dead but still walking around thinking they are alive. These are the people that hang on to outdated business models that were never effective to begin with.

Just as this book is not about sales, so the death of the salesman—the concept, not the play—is not about sales, either. For me the death of the salesman is analogous to the death of leadership. Effective leadership in today's business world has all but vanished, and the impacts are being felt everywhere. I am here to say that in corporate offices across the globe the dead and soon to be dead are roaming the hallways.

While this isn't a twisted horror story from the back catalogue of *The Twilight Zone,* in some ways it's more frightening. What makes a horror story truly terrifying, after all, is the idea that it could happen to you. Sadly, if you are working in business anywhere today, you are likely witnessing this story unfold around you. The good news is you can write a happy ending to the story. The bad news is it will come with some pain. And unless you value the reward more than the pain, it's not likely you will venture on the journey at all. It will take a challenge: your leadership challenge.

There are many factors contributing to the leadership gap which we will explore more closely in later chapters, but we'll touch on two primary ones here. One is something I call Business-Based Attention Deficit Disorder (BADD); the other is leadership atrophy.

Business leaders and the business schools that teach them have become overly enamored with too many processes and techniques, which has led to a predisposition toward BADD behaviors. At its root, BADD is enabled by data and distractions. Leaders tend to overemphasize data to the exclusion of truly meaningful information. One of my favorite expressions is, "If a company only knew what it knows." Sometimes the best information is right at our fingertips—our own staff and the knowledge they carry with them—and yet we are reluctant to access it by asking and listening. Listening skills and the willingness to work from a blank sheet of paper have become a lost art. This has become exacerbated with distractions brought on by technology-enabled communications: email, text messages, Twitter, and mobile access to the Internet. We live in the age of distractions.

The second factor contributing to the leadership gap is leadership atrophy. Many leaders fail to exercise key people skills such as building trust and developing relationships because they don't lead to near-term results. As these skills fall into disuse, they atrophy. As new leaders come up in organizations, they are inadvertently taught that relationship skills are nice to have but are ultimately unnecessary. When they don't see a need for them and don't see them modeled, new leaders often fail to learn relationship skills and, in turn, they fail to pass them on: hence the leadership gap.

The way to close the leadership gap is through leadership transformation—not cultural **change** foisted upon an organization but leadership *transformation* that flows through an organization organically. Before we can transform an organization, we need to transform ourselves. Sometimes this means letting go of how we did things in the past and opening ourselves to uncomfortable risk. Only after we evolve as leaders are we able to achieve transformation through new strategies, actions and solutions. The willingness to take this on is the leadership challenge.

The purpose of this book is to help leaders and potential leaders prepare themselves to meet this challenge, by understanding that the first step in leadership transformation is collaboration, not attempting to change the culture via command-and-control.

PLUS ÇA CHANGE, PLUS C'EST LA MÊME CHOSE

"Plus ça change, plus c'est la même chose" The more things change, the more they stay the same. Hundreds of books have been written on change management. Politicians run entire campaigns on change platforms, and I'm pretty sure you can get a post-graduate degree in change management. It's easy to see that the definition of change management is fairly broad. Business leaders define it in a variety of ways. For some, change is about breakthrough technology or invention. They're scanning the horizon for the next great idea, the next intergalactic product. Other leaders are more sophisticated about change. For them change isn't about products or services, it's about the underlying business model. Internet technology, for example, has dramatically impacted the book publishing industry. Witness the collapse of brick and mortar booksellers.

Still, for some leaders, change is rooted in geography. Take, for instance, when a company moves manufacturing units to countries where the economics are more favorable. Then there is the holy grail of all change: cultural change. How many times have you heard a business leader talk about changing the culture of an organization? They bring in consultants from around the globe to have brainstorming sessions, conduct stakeholder analysis and run benchmarking studies to confirm the data already collected. In the end, they come up with a set of platitudes underscored by impossibly complex protocols and processes and then brand it as change management.

But wait a minute, with all these change management books, degrees and initiatives covering all these different types of change, shouldn't businesses across the world be going gangbusters with growth and sales?

Could the reason businesses aren't thriving be that, despite all their efforts to change, they are simply implementing the same old solutions made over to look new? Could it be that these old solutions they're trying to dress up with the latest catchphrases and jargon aren't the right solutions, and that if the solutions failed to work in a sustained way in the past, they aren't likely to work today no matter how we rename them? Could it also be that despite all the changes in the marketplace, nothing has really changed at all? Perhaps people are still people, markets are still markets and the competition is still the competition. Plus ça change, plus c'est la même chose.

Instead of trying to change an organization, we need focus on transforming an organization. Now, if you haven't sensed this already, transformation is very different than change. Change is easy, sometimes superficial and short-lived. Transformation is difficult, runs deep and is long-lived.

In an organization, **change** comes about by how the business is managed: **transformation** comes about by how the business is led. Producing change requires no leadership involvement. To *change* an organization, leaders modify the way a business goes to market, they introduce improvements to existing products and they adjust coverage models. It's the same business working off the same base with some tweaks to grow volume and margin. To *transform* an organization, leaders pioneer a completely new business model, they introduce new and innovative products ahead of the competition or a market transition, they move a culture from command-and-control to teamwork-and-collaboration. Transformation is not simply a repositioning of the base; it is the creation of a new base.

An example is the above average athlete who transforms himself into a superstar via hard work and the application of new skills. The subtle difference is the mindset to transform into something better. It's having the leadership ability to focus and make the adjustments, external and internal, that will result in something better.

But transformation does not end once it has been achieved. Transformation is nothing if it cannot be sustained. Sports history is jam-packed with organizations that achieved greatness and then lost their way once the leadership disappeared. Each great leader had a belief that went beyond their discipline. For example, John Wooden preached being the best you can be and stated that if you gave all you had then the outcome of the game didn't matter. He never talked about winning or losing, just about achieving your full potential. John Wooden created a winning program while, unfortunately, the post-Wooden era has become all about winning. There are business leadership examples such as Gene Amdahl and Scott McNealy at Sun Microsystems who both started successful companies that eventually failed. Even Steve Jobs founded, left and was brought back to save Apple. Why did they succeed and then fail? I submit that one very significant factor was that the shift in leadership caused a shift in culture.

Leading through example and role modeling is extremely powerful and necessary when transforming an organization. Others see ideal behaviors and realize that they can maximize their potential in the same way. One leader can transform an organization with a vision of excellence or their strategic intent, but the test of real transformation is whether the new culture is able to sustain itself once the leader goes away.

Let me be clear. In talking about transformation we're not talking about creating world peace or putting a man on the moon, but we're also not talking about tactical change management. We're talking about a powerful internal transition that creates real leaders from the inside out and then impacts organizations in meaningful and lasting ways. To transform an organization we need to first transform ourselves as leaders. And that is no small order. It's probably the hardest thing leaders will ever have to do.

SNATCH THE PEBBLE FROM MY HAND

Anyone who was around in the '70s remembers the television show *Kung Fu*. In the opening sequence Kwai Chang's master tells him, "When you can take the pebble from my hand, it will be time for you to leave." When Kwai Chang finally achieves the task that allows him to leave, he then has to make his way in the Wild West of America. Analogously, business leaders today are making their way in the Wild West (and East) of a highly challenging landscape.

Now, Kwai Chang had two skills at his disposal. One was martial arts expertise; the other was spiritual insight. This is similar to today's leaders who have a choice between command-and-control leadership or a more open style like teamwork-and-collaboration. Just as Kai Chang resorted to fighting when backed into a corner, so business leaders resort to command-and-control when faced with difficult situations. "My way or the highway," becomes the rule of the day. In a business reality of unrelenting challenge, nine times out of 10 leaders are going to revert to command-and-control.

The skills leaders must learn to use are skills more akin to Kwai Chang's spiritual insights; skills that bias listening and connection over command-and-control. The difficulty is that leaders have become so reliant on command-and-control for so many years it has limited their ability to open themselves to true transformation.

When I consider the things that leaders feel are holding them back from transformation, I think of three conundrums leaders confront every day:

- **How do we get there from here?** While leaders have not necessarily lost sight of long-term value, they have lost sight of how to get there. Let's say things are worse than they have ever been. The economy has tanked, technology has changed the planet and no one plays fair any more. What has been the leadership response? Sadly, it's been fairly predictable: cut headcount, sell assets, focus on the basics and master the supply chain. It's the same tactics over and over again. Corporate leaders complain the world has changed and yet they insist on solving new problems with old thinking. They are building the future based on the past. This scenario of leveraging tried and true management techniques, but failing to upgrade leadership happens over and over again in the business world. Management techniques are great for enhancing the status quo but do not value the innovation required to truly grow any business. How do you drive innovation when you only have time to manage the business?

- **How do I embed vision in an organization?** Whether vision is foundational or groundbreaking, the problem is distilling it through all the levels of the organization so that it can be implemented, and so it can stick. Visions tend to get lost in the upper levels of leadership or, worse, morph into something completely unrecognizable by the time they hit the shop floor. What you end up with is an unaligned organization. It's very difficult to get where you need to go when members of your team are headed in a different direction.

- **How do we create true believers?** When people at any level of an organization don't believe in the vision, mission and strategy, the magic goes away. It's the premise of every Santa Claus story ever written. When the world stops believing in Santa, Christmas goes away. Let's take sales as an example. If a sales team believes in what they are selling, sales will be off the charts. All organizations need a critical mass of true believers.

Once you have true believers you seldom lose them. You can see the results when they have true belief in the same mantra, and you can see the results when they don't. It almost is like magic, or as we used to say in Chicago, FM—"friggin' magic!"

The material we cover in this book will help readers resolve these conundrums through means that are not always popular and not always talked about (in text books, business schools or boardrooms) but which I have found to be very effective.

WHAT TO EXPECT FROM THIS BOOK

Before we review the structure and content of the book, let us level-set expectations. First, this book is not a how to manual. If you are after a how to manual, you may want to put this book down and scan further down the aisle or refine your electronic search. While I offer some insights into leadership techniques and tools that have worked for me, the skill it takes to apply these depends on the reader's personal and professional experiences and their willingness to transform.

Transformation does not stem from reading a book. Transformation stems from conviction and behavioral courage. I can't magically transmit conviction and new behaviors or provide you with a smart pill. I can only share my own experiences and what I learned from them. The rest is up to you.

Second, I have found that stories are hugely important to communicate, and frankly, I enjoy telling them. I will substantiate my stories with real, actionable insights. I come from Chicago, from an age when direct talk, though sometimes unflattering and not so pretty, was valued more than eloquence. I will strive to be direct.

Now, if the reader is allowed expectations, it's only fair the author can have a few expectations as well. I have two expectations of you.

First, I expect my readers to do something. What I present here is a call to action. I will establish the burning platform, the imminent and unfortunate death of leadership as we once knew it, and I'll even show you a bridge to a better place. It's up to you to do something about it.

Second, I want you to take this book personally. True transformation starts from within. To transform an organization, you must first start with the leader. It's a sad fact that most leaders are more comfortable implementing change upon an organization than generating transformation within themselves.

REVIEW OF STRUCTURE

The flow of this book will follow my career as I progressed from an individual contributor to a manager to a leader. I structured the book in this way because it's how I learned my lessons and it seems right that I share my story in the same sequence it occurred for me. I also think this is the general track of most people's careers, and so you can easily place yourself in the context. And when I say story, I do mean story. I will illustrate and support many of my points with stories from my experience or the experiences of colleagues I have known throughout my career.

In the first section I'll tell the story of where I came from and how that shaped my leadership perspectives. I'll also establish exactly what the problem is we're trying to solve: defining the leadership gap, how it develops and its implications. In the second section we'll explore the distinction between science and art and how this is foundational to an individual's growth as a leader. In section three we'll delve more extensively into the art of leadership itself, including the key principles a leader needs to master. From there, we'll move into section four where we'll look at what it takes to transform a business. Finally, we'll examine the transformation that needs to occur within a leader before transformation can take root in an organization.

In the first chapter I'll take you to the north side of Chicago where I grew up. I'll share with you the ideas and values in which I was immersed in my college years at Northern Illinois University, and I'll bring you along on a few sales calls from my early career with A.B. Dick. Many of my ideas and views of sales, leadership and life come from this background and I think it's important to share some of my more salient impressions from those days. The underlying principle is that we never move too far away from where we were raised, metaphorically speaking. As leaders we need to come to terms with where we have been and understand how it has shaped us. Before transformation comes understanding.

In Chapter Two I'll delve into some key enablers of the leadership gap. Though I won't cover an exhaustive list, I'll look into three key dynamics, including push versus pull sales mentalities, atrophy, and the cost of free and good enough. I'll also reveal the scale of the problem. Simply put, the leadership gap isn't an issue facing small American businesses; it's an issue impacting international businesses with revenue in the billions. Also in this chapter I'll introduce Instant Replay sections at the end of each chapter, where I'll review key lessons and how they can be applied to leadership.

In section two, starting with the third chapter, I will review the science of selling, including sales calls and demos. You'll begin to get a glimpse of the art of selling. In parallel, I will touch on the science and art of leadership. During the process, I'll examine some of these ideas through simple formulas, which will be updated and expanded upon as you progress through other chapters.

We'll begin to explore leadership more directly in Chapter Four, where I'll establish a simple way of thinking about the art versus the science. As storytelling is a key tool in learning, I'll provide some experiences from my own background, as well as my colleagues', to better illustrate the concepts. Specifically, we'll look at how relationships play a key role in sales and leadership, how being vested in your customers' and employees' interests is better for a business than doggedly chasing your own interests, how not always having the answers can be a good thing and how acumen both in sales and in leadership can make all the difference. We'll round out the chapter by discussing the value of experience.

In section three we'll begin an extensive foray into the art of leadership. Beginning with Chapter Five I'll provide a view of the qualities and characteristics of a leader. As with other chapters, I'll demonstrate how these ideas look in real life by sharing stories from my own career as well as perspectives from colleagues.

In Chapter Six I'll offer some direct "be careful what you ask for" insights into leadership. In this chapter I'll cover concepts that are often overlooked but which every leader should learn to master, such as the blink tests and learning how to say "no" (at the right time). I'll also look at a phenomenon I refer to as "pipeline freeze," a topic most people can relate to but few people discuss. I'll also cover work-life integration and letting staff go. I'll end the chapter with some insights into executive presence.

Chapter Seven will test some age-old dichotomies such as strategies vs. tactics; delivery vs. activity; portfolio vs. project management; and finally teamwork-and-collaboration vs. command-and-control leadership styles. My conclusions may be surprising. To close the chapter I'll inquire into the issue of timing, particularly when it comes to vision, strategy and execution. My last topic will be the common pitfalls which create barriers and stumbling blocks to leaders.

After Chapter Seven I'll transition into the fourth section of the book where I'll address transforming an organization. Chapter Eight covers how to build strong teams. I'll start at the beginning of the people cycle and look at trends affecting the labor market, particularly how people today are managing their careers. I'll take a peek at how social networking impacts recruiting and how it's used by both by employers to scrutinize potential employees and vise-versa. After a discussion on recruiting, I'll dive into the interview process where I'll share some techniques I use to get past the mere science of interviewing, and get into the art of understanding the internal drivers of interviewees. Then I'll dive into the interview process and share techniques I use to go beyond the mere science of interviewing to understand the internal drivers of interviewees. In Chapter Nine I'll discuss some unique people development approaches.

In Chapter Ten I introduce the Collaborative Transformation Approach as a way to systematize transformation. Here I'll show you how to sift through the key components of transformation in an enterprise including leadership, governance, vision, strategy and execution. Of course you can't have a discussion about transformation without exploring culture, so I'll round off the chapter by showing how transformation depends, in large part, on establishing the right culture.

In Chapter Eleven I'll share my experience at Cisco in building the foundation for transformation with real, pragmatic change initiatives that delivered real, pragmatic results. Here I'll touch on how we identified issues that plagued the company, how we rallied the organization around building and delivering the solutions, and, since we do live in reality and not a fairy tale, I'll also share lessons we learned from our missteps.

Chapter Twelve will conclude our discussion on organizations. In this chapter I'll share some "tools of the trade" we used to institutionalize people development. Building on the premise that we play like we practice, as the staff becomes comfortable with using new communication tools and relationship building techniques, their skills in these areas will strengthen.

In section five I'll focus squarely on leadership transformation and how we can develop ourselves into better leaders and better people. In Chapter Thirteen I'll look at the power of intention as it applies to communication, businesses and our personal lives. To add color to the discussion I'll share a few stories about how intention in communication plays out when it is aligned and when it is misaligned. I'll also examine the impact intention can have on businesses through our words, through our behaviors and through the activities and actions we ask the organization to carry out. Most importantly, as leadership starts from within we'll test the role intention can and should play in our personal lives.

In the concluding chapter I'll think through another deep leadership concept—legacy. Intention guides action; legacy is the product of action. The leadership question becomes not only "What do you want your legacy to be?" but also "What will you do to leave that legacy?" Legacy, like intention, has to be purposeful and deliberate. In this final chapter I will provide some insights into what a legacy looks like and how it can be shaped. I will conclude with a challenge to my readers to develop and leave their own legacy in whatever endeavor they choose to lead.

YES, THERE WILL BE A TEST

Well, it's really more of a diagnostic tune up, a way to gauge where you are—though where you want to go is entirely up to you.

As a means to help one of my leadership teams, and myself, through a difficult transformation, I posed ten questions which we revisited over and over again as we strove to improve ourselves as leaders and as people. In one sense they are difficult questions, because to answer them with full transparency requires a certain degree of self-reflection.

My request to you is to ask yourself these questions. We won't be taking score—this isn't that kind of test. Note your answers below each question in the space provided. Keep these questions in mind as you read the book and refer back to them at the beginning of each section. Upon finishing the book, review your answers with someone you trust and commit to actions you will take to develop yourself in these areas.

....

1. *How do you see yourself in your peer group within your organization? Superior? Inferior? Equal? All of the above? Why?*

2. *Do you behave as if you belong on one team within your peer group?*

3. *Are you willing to put success of the team or organization above your personal success?*

4. *Do you work toward win-win results with your customers? Staff? Peers?*

5. *Do you take on the tough topics when they need to be taken on?*

6. *Do you know what factors within yourself may be inhibiting your own success?*

7. *Do you have confidence in yourself as a leader?*

8. *Do you instill trust in your customers? Staff? Peers?*

9. *Do you have credibility with your customers? Staff? Peers?*

10. *Do you have the desire to develop and improve your capabilities as a leader?*

OUR JOURNEY BEGINS

Thank you, reader, for picking up this book. Thank you for your attention and for taking this step on your leadership journey. For the next few hundred pages I am honored to be your guide. I began my journey many years ago when I took my first sales job at A.B. Dick. There was no way, even with a crystal ball or even a cherished Magic Eight Ball, for me to have known what adventures lay ahead. Today, so many years later, I still don't know what lies in the future, but I'm wiser from the journey and more ready than ever to forge ahead.

Let us begin . . . and remember to look for the Secret Sauce!

THAT WAS THEN, THIS IS NOW

"Do you know what my favorite part of the game is?
The opportunity to play."

—MIKE SINGLETARY

CHAPTER ONE

WHERE ARE YOU GOING, WHERE HAVE YOU BEEN?

My name is George O'Meara. I grew up on the north side of Chicago in the late 60's. Things were a lot different back then. For one, the urban sprawl was not quite as rampant as it is now, so when someone said they were from Chicago, it meant they were from the city. Today being from Chicago can mean anywhere from Naperville to Evansville, but I'm from Chicago, the city. In those days life was about being tough, frugal, and fast on your feet, sometimes literally. Those qualities were hardwired into me at an early age, and I carry them with me, for better or worse. As they say, "you can take the boy out of Chicago, but you can't take Chicago out of the boy." Chicago had an undeniable impact on me as a person as well as a leader. Some of the qualities instilled in me by that city have proven to be blessings, others hurdles. Either way, I wouldn't give any of it up.

FIREHOUSE BOXING

You are either from the north side or south side of Chicago. Along with the locale comes your affiliation—White Sox or Cubs fan. Technically since I was raised on the north side I should have been a Cubs fan, but since my dad grew up on the west side, the whole household was obliged to be Sox fans.

Chicago is known for several things—mobsters, pizza, blues and that big fire way back when. I don't know if it was because of that fire, but when I was growing up in Chicago there seemed to be a preponderance of firehouses. And every firehouse had a boxing ring. It seems unusual now, but it was the norm then. The men at the fire station were responsible for putting out fires across Chicago and for providing well-maintained boxing rings for the youth.

Knowing what to do with teenagers during the long, awkward transition from adolescence to adulthood is an age-old struggle. How do you work that angst out, how do you teach them humility, and how do you teach them to stand up for themselves? Back then the answer to all of these questions was at the firehouse. When I was 13 or so my dad told me, "You better learn how to defend yourself," and off to the firehouse I went.

Boxing was an effective way for a kid to toughen up. No matter how hard you tried, you were going to get hit and it was going to hurt. Boxing became an exercise in avoiding getting hit or hitting the other guy hard enough that he stopped hitting you. Either way, it didn't take long for the average teenager to learn the value of bob and weave and counter punch, throwing a quick left when there's an opening. Those 16-ounce gloves may look like cushy marshmallows, but after a few hits they feel like cinder blocks. And that sensation of your head snapping back like a bobble-head is no fun either. Kids learn quickly under those conditions.

In addition to toughening kids up, boxing also taught kids to face up to their problems. Once you were in the ring, there was no getting out unscathed. You had to face your adversary no matter how you felt about it. Today, I'm not so sure we teach our children that lesson, at least not as effectively as boxing rings did back then. Today it seems to be more about avoiding confrontation, thereby taking away the emotion as well as the experience. I'm a firm believer that we all learn the most under the pressure of the moment. Boxing instills a lot of that. Today you just don't see Mom dropping little Billy off at the boxing ring to spar for a few hours. It's off to soccer or lacrosse camps, which isn't a bad thing, but when people ask "What's the difference between the U.S. back then and the U.S. now?" that's one of them.

LIVE WHERE YOU WORSHIP,
LIVE WHERE YOU LEARN

My father insisted we live within walking distance of where we worshiped and where we learned. The first house we lived in was kitty-corner from our church and school. Our next house was less than two blocks away. My high school was just a block down from where I went to grammar school. But even at those short distances, walking to school could be hazardous to my health. Apart from the brutally cold winters, there were hooligans to deal with. In today's slang we'd call them something a little more crude, but the general idea is the same—these were kids who had too much time on their hands, too much to prove and too much of the idiot gene encoded in their DNA.

These hooligans would drive around armed with baseball bats and chains, flipping everyone off, trying to intimidate people and just basically being jerks. If you were hanging out with your friends and some of these other kids drove up . . . well, there was always a chance something was going to happen. The funny thing was, it always seemed that the littlest guy in the bunch would do the talking—there must have been something about being small that created a big mouth. The way it worked was that the little guy talked smack and the bigger guys did the stare down or, if things got out of hand, the head banging, literally. There was always some sort of standoff going on.

Even in school, kids were constantly being called out. My dad used to say, "Kid, if you know you're going to get into a fight, if it's really unavoidable, then you're better off throwing the first punch." I was always one to listen to my dad, and it seemed several times a month I was either going to detention or getting paddled with the "rod." Back then corporal punishment was the standard. The irony was that sometimes you'd get knocked around in a fight only to get popped with wooden rod from your teacher or principal. Then when your parents found out, smack down number three commenced (at least verbally). Some days you just couldn't win.

As you can imagine, growing up in the city necessitated a certain degree of survival skills. One of the best skills was to be part of the team. The adage, "safety in numbers," was literally true. Teams came in all sorts of shapes and sizes, but the most obvious teams were in pickup games of sports. In those times, playing sports was how we spent our free time, whether during recess, after school or on weekends.

There were selection methods for how you got on a team. They were the same methods kids use everywhere, even today. In basketball, for instance, the first one to make five free throws was picked and then the next and the next until you had ten players. Sometimes in a pick-up game at the local Y, you already knew all the players and the choices were based on past performances. Whoever was left ended up on the sidelines and watched. You learned quickly that if you wanted to be on the team and not be an onlooker, you had to sharpen your competitive edge. If you planned to play, you had to plan to win. One big lesson for me was that if I didn't have a plan I'd become part of someone else's plan. This lesson holds up in business, as well as sports and life.

The competitive edge wasn't just about sports. One of the most important skills you really had to master was how to bust someone's chops, and how to take having your own chops busted. Whenever you met someone new, you were obliged to throw a few verbal jabs to see how they reacted. If they came back with their own zingers and held their own, they had a chance to make the team. If they didn't, it was the "social sidelines" for them. It might sound harsh, but those were the unspoken rules that everyone played by. Life in Chicago was one constant boxing ring, in the verbal as well as physical sense.

I don't want to give the impression that Chicago was gang infested, but there were gangs and fights and a constant edge to everyone and everything. Compared to today's gangs, however, they were nowhere near as lethal. The fights were mostly fair, chains and bats excluded. All in all, it was a great place to be from, but it was also a *hard* place to be from.

The enduring lesson I learned from those Chicago days was that you don't run away from adversity, you step up to it and have the courage to face it head-on. If you prepare yourself, you're less likely to get hurt. You learn how to take the punches and to throw a few back. Likewise, in the business world you won't get far if you collapse under pressure and walk away from challenges. Have no doubt, the world of business is every bit as tough as North Chicago in the 1960s, but unfortunately in the business world there are no fire stations with boxing rings to help you learn how to cope.

A PENNY IS A PENNY

We didn't have much money when I was growing up, but money wasn't something that kids really worried about back then. You lived where you lived, you dressed how you dressed, and no one had iPads or Xboxes or laptop computers, so there was not as much of the "keeping up with Joneses" as there is today, at least not for the kids. You might say everyone was equally deprived.

Both of my parents worked. My Irish grandmother would come over and watch us kids after school. My father grew up in the depression, and his father died young. Growing up during the depression left an indelible mark on my dad. For him a penny was a penny and was not something to be wasted. I remember he used give me a soda or a glass of evaporated milk and say, "Kid," (he always called me kid, even when I was an adult) "Sip on it. Make it last." The point was I better enjoy it and appreciate what I had because there wasn't going to be seconds.

Did I say evaporated milk? My dad helped to make reconstituted milk a staple in American households. He'd buy those milk flakes, mix in some water and that was our milk. To use the vernacular, it tasted like crap, but it was affordable and that was that. He and my mother had six kids to look after. You can imagine what the milk bill could add up to. He didn't deprive us of our dairy, but I'm not sure what was worse—getting paddled at school or having to drink evaporated milk at home.

Frugality for frugality's sake was not my dad's brand of thrift; his was steeped in practical wisdom. I recall leaving the house one Saturday to go the Arlington race track. He stopped me at the front door as I was leaving. "Kid, can you do me one favor before you go? Can you go upstairs to your room, open the window nice and wide and just toss all your money out. You'll save yourself some time and suffering because that's exactly what's going to happen at the track."

My dad's frugality rubbed off on me. But it wasn't just my dad's frugality, it was generational. It started with the parents, was handed down to kids and infused everything. Those aren't habits and dispositions you shake overnight. It would be an interesting study to see how that mindset of frugality shaped Chicago business in those years. While I can't speak for society, I can speak for myself. Because of my upbringing, I mind every cent, hold to every budget and work to stretch the most value out of every asset I am allotted. It started with a glass of evaporated milk and is still paying dividends today.

THE FAST AND THE FURIOUS

I was the youngest boy in my family, with two brothers and three sisters. Growing up, I always tagged along with my older brothers and their friends. I grew up playing basketball, baseball, softball, football, golf—everything my brothers played, I played. Thankfully, I was blessed with great hand-eye coordination and reasonably good agility which helped me to keep up. When you have to "post up" against kids who are four to five years older, you learn a lot of skills the bigger guys never learn. Either you step up or fold. This is where I learned to watch, adapt and improvise; this is where I learned that what may look like a disadvantage can actually be an advantage because most kids don't like playing against older (tougher) competition. This lesson has served me well through life.

Another distinctive thing about Chicago was the alleys. These spaces—18 feet deep and as wide as a standard one car garage—became our gymnasiums. We'd play three-on-three, four-on-four, five-on-five basketball in these tight spaces. There, equal doses of finesse and brute force played out. I must have shot hoops, played horse (or 21) for 10 to 15 hours a week. Today, of course, kids put that much time in on video games over the weekend alone. I'm sure there's a skill kids pick up there, too, but it's hard to see how it stacks up against vigorous outdoor activities.

I should also say that my siblings were as smart as they were athletic. My grandfather had a photographic memory and I inherited a bit of that, which helped me do well in school. My brothers and sisters, however, were the real deal. They were the ones that set the high end of the curve in their classes. Other students must have hated them. I envied them because I was always in the half of class that made the upper half possible. For me, there were all sorts of expectations set by my parents and teachers who knew my siblings. Academically, I was under tremendous pressure to excel.

When I sum up these experiences, it's all about learning street smarts from the firehouses, sports and school. "Street smarts" is a type of wisdom that trains up your gut reactions, your intuition. Street smarts is about how and when to apply academic and social lessons.

BECOMING COACHABLE

In addition to the influence of my siblings in sports and academics, coaches were another major influence on me. Through them I learned to be coachable. When learning any sport, there are the right and wrong ways to execute a blocking assignment, run a pass route or read a defense. A good coach provides immediate feedback, negative as well as positive. I learned that "you play like you practice" and "feedback is the breakfast of champions." In sports as well as business and life, if you can't learn to take feedback, you won't learn and you won't become better. What you will have is a difficult time succeeding in sports, in the workplace and in life.

Lessons about the small things can become big life lessons. I remember when I was a sophomore playing Division I football at Northern Illinois University. I went home one weekend to visit a girlfriend. I got a ride to Chicago on Friday and had to take a Greyhound bus back to Northern on Sunday. I ended up getting to the Sunday night film session with the football team a good 30 minutes late. When my coach asked me why I was late, I stammered and was evasive. I knew extra sprints and benches were in store for me.

Now, Coach was the archetypal coach. He liked to get about two inches from your face and he had a tendency to shout when he wanted you to really pay attention—and apparently we must have had some attention deficits because he shouted a lot. His fingers were like mini tree stumps, so when he poked you in the chest it was like being hit by a battering ram. Coach pulled me aside, started talking so I could hear him real well and poking me with his battering ram fingers. He said "George, never ever try to defend your screw ups. Just own up to it and take your medicine." The lesson was a valuable one. It was about accountability, about taking ownership for your own actions, especially the mistakes. I have never forgotten that lesson. I even teach it to my kids, though with a different twist and without all the shouting. "The only way to get yourself out of a hole," I tell them, "is to stop digging." The funny thing is, when they see me digging myself into a hole, they start making shovel motions.

If executed properly, every play in football should accomplish exactly what it set out to do. If it is an offensive play and all 11 players do their job, they score a touchdown; if it's a defensive play, they stop the offense for a five yard loss.

Obviously, life doesn't always happen that way. People are people and they make mistakes. There are so many variables and any single thing that goes awry can blow the play. I learned that sometimes despite all the practice hours, or maybe because of all the practice hours, you don't always win. This is probably perfectly obvious to everyone—someone always has to lose. The point is, however, you do not actually plan to lose; rather you plan and practice to win! The ironic thing is, we have the opportunity to learn the most when we lose. A lot of people just lose and go on, and miss the lesson. That's true of sports as well as business and life.

SWEET HOME, CHICAGO

Northern Illinois University was far enough from home for me to feel independent, but close enough for me to feel safe—and to get some laundry done and grab a nice home-cooked meal during weekend excursions. While I wasn't raised by June and Ward Cleaver, I'd wager my mother could out cook Betty Crocker any night and my dad might as well have been Daniel Boone, at least in my eyes. The fact that my mother was a tremendous cook is nothing compared to the goodwill she put into the community. The fact that my dad could weave captivating tales from common observations paled compared to the energy he put into being a role model for his children. My dad was a salesperson and I went into sales, which is a telling fact. I'm not just waxing nostalgic. My parents had a kind of magic and I'm not ashamed to say I used that magic more than once.

I already mentioned a girlfriend I would go to see in Chicago. Well, through my college career I had several girlfriends. Now, I was no Don Juan. These were serial monogamous relationships. So here's the true confession. In college, whenever I met a girl that I really wanted to impress, whose esteem I just couldn't quite capture well enough, I'd take her home to meet my mom and dad. My parents would meet us at the door. My dad, "the ambassador" as my friends called him, would reach out to my date with that firm reassuring handshake, wrapping his other hand round the top and gazing into her eyes with his own deep steely-blue eyes. My mom would greet her with her warm smile, a hug and attentive listening skills.

With the ambiance of a home-cooked meal and the loving atmosphere my parents naturally created, no girl stood a chance but to fall madly in love with . . . my parents. On one hand, it's a sad witness to the desperation of a college student; on the other, it's a touching testimony of the genuine charisma of my parents. While I cannot say my parents' charm was enough to completely win over a girl on my behalf, I will say that without a doubt my deepest and most lasting lessons of emotional intelligence came from my mother and my father.

YASGUR'S FARM

Not long ago I had the chance to take one of my sons on a tour of Haight-Ashbury in San Francisco. As we were touring the famous flower-power sights, my son started asking me questions about those years. I told him about Tom Hayden, the Students for Democratic Society, protests I attended and why it was all such a big deal. I was a college sophomore on May 4th, 1970, when the Kent State incident occurred. There were riots and protests and cars getting flipped over and burned at campuses across the US.

It was news to him that I was ever remotely aware of, much less involved with, these types of landmark occurrences. My son stepped back, looked at me and said, "What? I thought you were this white guy who works for this major corporation with your button downs and ties."

In his mind's eye he was seeing images of long-haired hippies, Jimi Hendrix at Woodstock and Janis Joplin in Golden Gate Park. The sports-playing, milk-drinking college dad he knew just didn't fit in the picture. It took him the rest of that afternoon to come to terms with the idea that people change—and that he may change as well—and that although people may change their outward appearances for the sake of employment and the general pressures of an orderly society, most people hold on to their inner values. The fact is, you can buy in and still not sell out. From my experience, there are a lot of seemingly straight-laced, uptight corporate types that are really hippies inside.

Alongside the lessons I learned from playing sports and from the tough streets of Chicago, I also learned about standing up for what you believe, questioning when something has gone astray and championing the less fortunate. These are powerful leadership lessons when held in the right context.

When I talk about my formative years, it sounds like I took on these great life-altering insights and never looked back. The truth is, by the time I graduated from college those lessons were just starting to percolate inside me. I was very much a work in process. It took 20+ years for many of those lessons to take hold. I was a highly competitive, driven, no-holds-barred son-of-a-bitch, and a lot of companies I worked for rewarded me handsomely for that type of behavior. I'm not necessarily proud of this, but it is the path I took, and fortunately I learned enough along the way to make several course corrections.

A DAY IN THE PATCH

In 1973, as a new college graduate with a BS in marketing, I made my way down to 110 North Wacker to the branch office of my new employer, A.B. Dick, the copier, duplicator, mimeograph and printing machine company.

Most sales offices in those times were structured the same. I walked into the receptionist area and then past the demo room, otherwise known as "the magic room" because that is where all the magic happened. Then I passed the executive offices and boom, way in the back there it was: the bullpen. At 70'x50', it was four times as big as the ally we used to play ball in at home, and instead of a basketball hoop there were desks and file drawers stuffed with order pads, brochures, customer files and records. Oh, and there were phones everywhere. This was clearly well before the cell phone era.

For the next three years that bullpen was my home, or at least my home base, because back then my real home was on the road meeting clients, cementing relationships, sealing deals. From June 20th, 1973 until I left A.B. Dick I would walk into that bullpen every morning. The guys would be beating on the phones and then suddenly around 8:00 am, everybody would be gone. It was death to be in the office after 8:30. The bullpen was the place you'd go to set up your appointments for the rest of the day, and then you'd be out there pressing the flesh and making colds calls.

The only two weeks I didn't start my day in the bullpen were the two weeks I went to sales training at our headquarters in Skokie. The instructors would teach and hammer us every day. They were god-like in answering every objection, presenting any pitch, and recalling every product speed and feed. They were flawless in their demos. These guys were former district or regional managers who wanted to go into corporate management. Sales training was the interim step where they paid their dues, and they were set on succeeding.

It was during those weeks that I was again reminded to "play like you practice." We had to role-play sales calls in front of our peers with these intense instructors who had seen every twist and had an encyclopedic knowledge of everything sales related. Keep in mind this is a hyper competitive crowd doing something that for most of us did not come naturally. The pressure was immense. Invariably we'd make mistakes; it felt like your every flaw was on display for your peers to see.

The thing about this kind of exercise is that the class can collectively out-think you by a margin of 2 to 1. That is, for every second it takes to process information, catch a twist, call out an objection, the class can figure it out in half the time. You want to make those mistakes in practice and not in the game. When you make mistakes in practice, at worst it's embarrassing, and you learn a valuable lesson. When you make mistakes in the field you lose a sale, the competition gains one up on you and you have to work extra hard to hit your quota.

So here's how it plays out in the field. You get into your car in the morning after checking into the bullpen. It is 95° in Chicago, which means the humidity is only lagging by a few percentage points. You're in a suit and tie, hefting a sample bag. You get to your first stop. It's a cold call. You make the 300 steps to the front door across sweltering asphalt. As you push open the office doors you see the big red sign that reads "no soliciting." It was 95° outside; it's 69 inside. Every drop of sweat turns to ice. You walk up to the receptionist.

"Hi, I'm here to talk about your communications needs."

The receptionist looks up from her paperwork. "What?"

You clear your throat and straighten your shoulders a bit. "I'm here to talk about your office copier. I'm wondering if you are happy with your copier or if you need any supplies?"

Eyebrows lift up. "What?"

Deep breath. "Can I please talk to the office manager or someone in purchasing?"

You have this whole presentation and demo worked out and you're stuck at the receptionist's desk. It is very hard to make a sales call from that vantage point. The reality is, before you win over the boardroom you need to first win over the receptionist. And every good receptionist has a well-deserved Ph.D. in bullshit detection. There's no bluffing at the front desk.

It has been a total of 93 seconds since you stepped into the office and you are back on the sweltering asphalt, the door swinging closed behind you. You head to cold call number two. Maybe you do a little better and you pull off a full two minutes. You find a diner, grab a cup of coffee and call into the bullpen for your messages. You got a call from ACME Appliance on 550 W. Madison. The office manager has a problem with his copier. He wants to know if you can help. Now you have an appointment. Things are looking up.

You walk in. The receptionist is expecting you. You walk past the rows of desks to the manager's office.

As you are walking in, you recall another cold call experience where all twenty of the employees stopped what they were doing and looked up at you like you were Clint Eastwood stepping into the Lonely Dog saloon. And then the purchasing agent, who really believed he *was* Clint Eastwood, was summoned from his quarters. You could have heard a pin drop, or at least a pen click, as he sauntered up to you in the lobby. While there are rooms set aside to have discussions, he wanted to have this talk right there in the open where he could be seen. So you had to do your pitch in front of all the other waiting salespeople. Good thing you practiced.

Back in the present, the receptionist rapped lightly on the door and eased her head in. "Mr. /Ms. 'Fill in the Blank' is here to see you." She smiled at you and opened the door. It's a comfortable office.

More flashbacks to contrast: You recall a sales appointment with Mr. Big. You walked into the palatial office. Mr. Big's desk was 30 feet away from where you had to sit. His desk was about 40 inches tall and the couch you sank into was about six inches off the floor. Your butt was lower than your knees. He said, "What would you like to talk about, Son?" It was like talking to the Wizard of Oz.

But this sales call with ACME Appliance was much different. The manager put down the phone and extended a hand as you stepped up to the desk. You started your pitch and he was all ears. For the moment you were golden.

Day by day, you experienced a range of emotions and circumstances that took you from beggar to king and back again. It was all about timing, luck, and learning to get by the receptionist. It was all about having the right solution for the right problem. Over time, you relaxed into your role. You became versed in the science of selling. You started seeing the syntax of each sales call, and learning from your mistakes. You started gathering a storehouse of experience to draw from. You glimpsed the art of selling.

BEAUTIFUL CLOCK

During sales training at A.B. Dick, one of the techniques they taught us was to look for something on the wall or desk of a prospect's office and comment on it to help establish rapport. I can remember being on a sales blitz. A sales blitz is when you team up with another salesperson, pull up a zip code and start hitting every potential business. You go up and down, two inches deep, 80 miles an hour through the entire zip code. So I was teamed up with a colleague and, at this one office we got past the receptionist. We walked into the operation manager's office. I looked up and I saw an elaborate clock. I said, "That's a really beautiful clock."

I should say I knew nothing about clocks except how to read time, but I knew enough to notice that clock stood out like a museum piece in an otherwise plain office. It obviously meant something to the prospect. All I had to do was express genuine interest and from there we had an authentic conversation. The tactic worked, and eventually we got around to talking about the copiers, and she ended up putting in a sizable order.

As we left the office, my colleague turned to me and said, "O'Meara, a beautiful clock? Where'd you get that one from?" From then on whenever we made a great sale we'd call it a "beautiful clock sale."

Months later we'd be at the bar recapping the day and someone would say, "Man, I had a great sale today!"

"A beautiful clock sale?"

"Not quite, but it was pretty awesome . . ."

That was when I learned the key to a successful sales call is "connecting" with your client. These connections have to start somewhere. The most obtuse frame of reference isn't a bad place to start. Another great place to start is with common references. For instance, one of my favorite cars is a 1969 Chevelle SS 396. If someone were to tell me a printer could crank out copies as fast as a SS 396, I'd be in their pocket. As the expression goes, "you are now what you were then"—that is, the likes and dislikes you had in your formative years are likely to be the preferences you hold on to for life. In my case, I am still that kid from the North side of Chicago who grew up in the 60's and 70's.

If a salesperson knew the preferences of their prospects or customers, they could tap in to an untold treasure of emotional hooks. Creating genuine connections is an art that you have to layer on to the technical aspects of selling.

THE THREE COINS

The Three Coins Café was on North Wells Street at Randolph. Some days a bunch of us would leave the bullpen and head over to the Coins. We'd order up some breakfast and coffee and start shooting the bull. We'd share war stories about, "beautiful clock sales," purchasing agents who were jerks and tips from the road. Every hour we'd check our messages from the phone booth. Sometimes there would be nothing; other times a lead or an appointment. All of a sudden it would be 10:30, 11:00, 12:00—time for lunch. Off to another spot, grab something to eat, more phone calls, more stories. Soon it would be four o'clock, and we'd head off to a place called the Sub Pub on Wacker. Every day they would have different specials, but the standard was "doubles for a buck." There we'd have more talking, more sharing, and more relationship-building.

One of the neat things about Chicago life, and this still holds true today, is the tavern life. Drive around anywhere in the Chicagoland area and you'll see taverns and microbreweries everywhere. They're usually deceptively spacious and warmly insulated. The cold of the winters tends to drive people indoors, so these taverns are made to make you feel cozy and comfortable just like an extension of your living room. Back then every four blocks or so there'd be a tavern or gin mill. Just like in England where every village has a pub or three, in Chicago every neighborhood had its own tavern. Our tavern was Danny's at the corner of Belmont and Austin. Each Tavern had it's beer—Pabst Blue Ribbon, Schlitz, Budweiser, Old Style, Hamm's—and each had pool tables and sometimes electronic bowling. They also had that big, long mahogany bar, the kind that most people want to replicate in their homes or basements today.

Taverns weren't just about drinking, though. The local tavern was where you learned about relationships. At the end of the day you'd somehow wind up at the local tavern with your pals. You'd either arrive with them or they'd just start to show up. You could walk into any one of those places, put down a double sawbuck to buy a round for everyone and still have change. Since you bought one round, someone else would buy the next, someone else the next and so on and so on. Many hours later you're walking out after a full night of shooting pool and shooting the bull with your friends. You'd share whatever happened to you that day, talk about your hopes, your dreams, your failures—anything and everything. This is where you really learned about people and those you chose to call your real friends. My dad always said, "Kid, if you end up with one or two real friends in your lifetime you will be blessed." I'm glad to say I'm on track to being blessed.

Starting the day with breakfast at the Three Coins Café wasn't an everyday occurrence, but it happened often enough. The thing was, during all that time spent with colleagues and friends, we were swapping tactics and customer experiences. More importantly, we were learning to bond, build relationships, and how to make connections. I learned from boxing rings, alleys, football fields, from family. I learned from the bullpen, from crash and burn calls, from beautiful clock sales, and from the Three Coins. The world is our classroom. We just need to make sure we show up and pay attention.

CHAPTER TWO

WHEN PUSH COMES TO SHOVE

Before I go much further with my story, I'd like to pause a moment to describe the environment in which the leadership gap has grown. In this chapter, we'll explore three powerful dynamics out of the possibly hundreds that over the years have worked to enable the leadership gap: the push vs. pull paradigm, atrophy and the cost of free.

The world in which I launched my career was in flux. I was fortunate, however, in that I had a privileged career—not privileged in the sense of managed moves or cushy positions, but privileged in the sense of who I worked with, who coached and mentored me, and who influenced me. These people helped me to circumvent the leadership gap—or at least scramble out of it before I had fallen too far. I think if I had been wise enough at the time I could have seen the leadership gap evolving around me. When you are in the toxic grasp of the dynamics that we are going to explore in this chapter, and when you are surrounded by command-and-control managers, it is hard to recognize the issues at hand; however, each one of these gap-making forces creates an opportunity for growth *if* you decide to pay attention and learn from those experiences.

PUSH AND PULL

The tension between "push" and "pull" sales models has helped to define the leadership gap. In the "push" sales model, negotiating deals becomes a means to build volume. Here, a seller foists goods and services onto a potential buyer and entices them with price reductions or hard-sell tactics. They do this because their competition can offer similar products at similar prices. The ability to sell hard and fast becomes a matter of survival.

In the customer's eyes, push salespeople are unsophisticated purveyors of commodities. With the advent of the Internet and an unprecedented access to information, the role of the push salesperson is becoming increasingly obsolete. As a result, more of the push salesperson's role is migrating to the web. Only the largest customers will have direct salespeople, and they are only there to provide a single point of contact for the customer.

A classic example of the push sales model is the automotive industry. If I'm in the market for a new car, I can research it online, compare models side-by-side and find who has the best price—everything I would have relied on a salesperson to tell me, and more, is right at my fingertips almost instantly. The only impact the salesperson has on the sale is price negotiation—that is, how much margin they are willing to give up in order to land the sale.

Today, those stuck in the push space are finding it a difficult proposition. With push techniques come a stigma of mistrust. Customers put all vendors in a "box," classifying them into one of several categories. (Of course, it is the salesperson that actually puts themselves in a box and not the customer.) Here's a rundown of some common boxes salespeople find themselves in:

- **Transactional vendors** push their products as the one-size-fits-all solution. Their goal is to meet their quota at all costs. Transactional vendors are hardcore push dealers.

- **Innovation gurus** see product innovation as the cure-all. They depend on cutting-edge technologies and encourage their customers to become early adopters. They are future focused and tend to promise solutions tomorrow though the problem may exist today. Innovation gurus are push salespeople.

- **Price contenders** focus on return on investment for the customers through the commercial value-add their product will provide or through the low cost they can secure. Either way, they contend on current price or future returns. Price contenders are push salespeople.

- **Average Joes** are reliably great on some things and just as reliably poor on others. For instance, they may provide great product support but have terrible technical specs. Average Joes can be push or pull salespeople.

- **Best friends** overdo relationship building. They are great people but tend to be conciliatory and have a difficult time making decisions. They always agree with the customer but are unable to make things happen on the customer's behalf. Best friends can be push or pull salespeople but are typically ineffective as either.

- **Experienced advisors** invest themselves in the customer's business. They strive to understand the customer's environment and provide solutions that are focused on the customer's business objectives. They challenge assumptions and are not afraid to say when they cannot provide a solution or when they think their solution is just average, even if it means losing a sale. Experienced advisors are pull salespeople.

The experienced advisor box, obviously, is the place to be. The other boxes, however, are problematic. Once in a problematic box, it's tough to get out. To get out you will have to move the mountain of customer perception. They say to move a mountain you must first believe you can move a mountain. I would add that to move a mountain you also have to be willing to try. Why would someone be unwilling? Because to get out of the box, to move the mountain, requires not only a change of external behaviors but a transformation of internal values. A lot of people find that much transition too difficult to take on.

In the "pull" sales model, customers are drawn into a sale based on a product's benefits that deliver value according to the customer's needs. Oftentimes the needs are latent and it is the salesperson who surfaces them. In a pull model it is almost as if the customer is allowed to buy instead being sold. Push connotes a stick approach, pull suggests a carrot.

As an innovative way of pull-selling, technology consultant and author Geoffrey Moore promotes a technique he calls "provocation selling." In provocation selling the salesperson works with the customer to determine where business processes are losing money and will continue to do so unless they act to stem the bleeding. In this way, the customer discovers where they can "create budget" which would "self-fund" the solution. If the problem they had would stop bleeding money, they could afford the solution being offered. This is the classic "sell the problem, sell the solution" model. A "transactional vendor" would push a product or service regardless of the problem, a "best friend" salesperson would do whatever the customer wanted, regardless of the potential outcomes; but an experienced advisor would not be afraid of introducing challenge and soliciting the customer in determining the solution.

As an example of how opposing "push" and "pull" models work, let's look at the mainframe industry. When mainframes were new, the primary role of the push salesperson was to educate the customer on the new technologies, showcasing the benefits over older technologies and the potential for those improvements to advance the customer's interests. The point was to convert the customer to the new technology. Mainframe technologies, however, soon became commoditized. Systems were on par with one another, the differentiating points flattened and pricing became the last frontier on which companies could compete. Efforts were poured into monetizing softer benefits such as customer service and brand halo effects. Here the push salesperson competed for sales through features, advantages and contract negotiations.

In this push world, information became king. Value shifted from the actual technology, or products that hosted it, to intelligence on technology. And the intelligence provider had to be reliable, accurate and trusted. Customers began to depend on analysts such as Gartner to provide advice and guidance on technologies and price. These analysts became experienced advisors to the customers while the vendors they recommended were left to negotiate deals. These intelligence providers became the first wave of mainframe technologies pull salespeople.

To succeed, advisors had to create a relationship with customers. First, they had to become vested in the customer's problems. If they were going to suggest technological solutions, they had to know what issues the customers were facing, what kept them up at night, how much they were willing pay to get a good night's rest and, more importantly, they had to be in front of where the customer wanted to go. Traits of the experienced advisor were, and still are, as follows:

- **Customer focused:** The experienced advisor understands their customer's business as well as their own. They are vested in helping the customer grow their business.

- **Vendor agnostic:** The experienced advisor's only interest in a vendor is their ability to meet their customer's needs.

- **Strategically minded:** The experienced advisor has a deep understanding of the big picture and being "in front" of where the customer wants to go, including the external and internal pressures, constraints, advantages and capabilities. The experienced advisor knows where the customer needs to go and has an executable plan to get them there.

- **Tactically savvy:** The experienced advisor can provide solutions to complex business issues and break them down into manageable implementation phases within the customer's constraints (i.e. cost, time, resources).

- **Relationship skilled:** The experienced advisor builds and maintains an earnest and authentic relationship with his/her customer, which is based on helping the customer meet their strategic objectives.

To its credit, in the early 1990's, IBM met the problem of transforming its sales force into experienced advisors head-on. In the heyday of the mainframe era, IBM dominated the technology product space. But their position fell to more nimble competitors and the company split into two segments—the products segment and the services segment. The services segment became IBM Global Services, which supports any technology that the customer needs. Here's how IBM describes their Global Business Services on their website:

> *Our business consulting practice brings together a powerful combination of functional and industry expertise required to take full advantage of the opportunity presented by digital transformation. Whether it is reshaping your*

business strategy, operating model or optimizing your entire supply chain, our experienced Strategy & Transformation consultants can help.[1]

The keys words here are "expertise," "transformation" and "help." Granted we can write this off as consultancy speak, but the point is that IBM once competed on products and they now compete on services—and they do it from a relationship platform. The benefits they bring to bear are *how* they interface with customers to arrive at solutions the customer needs, as opposed to pushing products IBM is looking to sell.

In a products business the client relationship is centered on the product's features, advantages, and benefits. In the mainframe era, relationships were all about the products. When technology changed, the basis of those relationships also changed. The conversation was no longer about what distinctive features one particular product had over the competition's product, but rather a question of price.

> *"I believe the 'push' is the wrong strategy for this decade and for the century ahead of us. I think we need to be in an invite mindset. I think the new world says we need to invite people to consider, invite people to share with us, invite them to join us in a discussion that will help solve their problems. We need to come from a point of curiosity as sales professionals rather than a point of push. I think the old mindset was push and the new mindset is invite."*
>
> —MIKE STAVER, CEO, The Staver Group

To contrast, in a services business, the relationship is based on people. As technology changes, the relationship remains. Of course, if you are in the products business it is not likely you can drop your assets and move completely into the services business, but you can certainly diversify, which is exactly what IBM did. IBM is not the only company in this arena. There are Accenture, Bain, Boston Consulting Group, McKinsey, and the list goes on.

---

[1] "How IBM Can Help." IBM Global Services. IBM. Web. 24 Sept. 2011.
http://www-935.ibm.com/services/us/gbs/consulting/.

So what happened to the mainframe salesperson that is still competing on price and value add? Typically on one tier the customer is using an experienced advisor who recommends the product vendor. On the lower tier the product vendors are competing on price and falling victim to the race to zero. Sadly, most companies on the lower tier had no idea what was happening when the products to services bifurcation happened. They placed their faith in transactional selling and their customer base shifted to those practiced experienced advisors. As those customers shifted, the premium margin shifted with them.

The leadership implication here is twofold. First, a leader can choose to base a company's customer-facing sales organization on a push model or a pull model.

The push model is easily implemented, though short-lived. The pull model is much more intricate but longer-lived. Second, as the dynamic of "push" and "pull" exist in sales, so they exist in leadership. A leader can choose to head their organization with push management tactics, otherwise known as command- and-control, or through pull leadership tactics, otherwise known as teamwork-and-collaboration.

ATROPHY LEADS TO ENTROPY

The second dynamic that has helped shape the leadership gap is atrophy. In biological terms, atrophy occurs when we fail to exercise a muscle group to the point that the muscle group begins to weaken and deteriorate. The same thing happens in sales, in leadership, and in life. Behaviors and values we fail to use just slip away.

Let's focus on how atrophy deteriorates the world of sales. From there we can build corollaries into leadership. As noted earlier, much of the business world exists on a landscape flattened by the effects of commodity sales. Technology has played a large role in this flattening, with salespeople becoming more practiced in taking orders over the Internet and working against a fixed price rather than discussing customer needs and working with clients to discover solutions. Some companies are advancing rapidly in automating the more labor intensive aspects of customer relationship management. Here are several dynamics that add to the atrophying of sales:

- **Training:** Most organizations and salespeople are quite adept at mastering "push" or transactional selling. Because transactional selling is more tangible and measurable, it gets taught in formal training programs. "Pull" selling, on the other hand, is often considered a natural talent, something that can't be trained and can only be picked up by "getting old"—that is, through years of experience. It is also often considered a "soft" skill, a behavior to be absorbed as opposed to knowledge to be taught. In this most likely scenario, transactional sales techniques are taught and "pull" techniques are ignored.

- **Capacity:** Many people simply don't have the capacity, the interest or the time to get beyond the technical aspects of sales. We have all seen the employee, for example, who is an incredible tactician but for the life of them just cannot wrap their heads around strategy. The same applies for sales—some people excel at the "push" selling but are never able to expand past it. It's not that they are poor performers; they may be excellent at what they do, but they never grow. They, and their managers, eventually become the Willy Lomans of the world, holding on to ineffective sales models while the world sails by.

- **Line of least resistance:** Transactional selling is easy. A salesperson will learn the fewest steps necessary to land an order and they will follow those steps every time. Becoming an experienced advisor can be complex and unsure, as well as difficult to forecast. At times you need to risk the sale in order to make the sale, and risk represents more steps and inherent uncertainty.

- **Inertia of linearity:** A sales culture of linearity creates an organizational drive to keep delivering short-term results. It's hard to plan out the game when you are tied up in a constant stream of "dive and catch" plays where in the last minute of a desperate situation one high-performer makes a stunning effort and wins the day. In a culture of linearity, the sales force is focused on making this week's, month's or quarter's committed sales; leadership is focused on making sure that is what the sales force is focused on. Everyone has their head down and leadership is commanding the charge. It's an illusion to think that increases in sales from intense short-term drives are permanent, because the market can shift, the economy can tank, and products can become commodities. It will be time to exercise a different type of sales muscle, but companies will realize too late (or not at all) that their true sales muscles have atrophied.

Pulling all these scenarios together, it's easy to see how atrophy can take root. Atrophy leads to entropy and in entropy an organization's collective ability to compete deteriorates.

In my experience, sales skill atrophy, or the "Loman Virus," can spread like a pandemic. Through a causal chain of influence, leaders, managers, direct reports, peers, colleagues, and trainees all share their science-centric mindset. An entire company can quickly slip into sales atrophy by simply building the future based upon the past. When those people move on to other companies, the gap in sale skills spreads alarmingly fast. Since "push" selling is so deeply codified in institutional memory via training manuals, text books and other media, those basic skills are in less danger of atrophy. The more esoteric, behaviorally based skills are the ones in danger of becoming extinct; and if this happens in sales, think about what can happen in leadership. The reality is that critical leadership skills, beyond command-and-control techniques, also are seldom taught through training programs; few new leaders desire them (because they aren't incentivized and they aren't role-modeled); they are difficult to implement; and they rarely lead to short-term results. The truth is our workforce of today is littered with Willy Lomans who are generating replicas of themselves—outmoded, outdated and out-skilled, not only in sales skills but in leadership.

THE COST OF FREE AND GOOD ENOUGH

The third and final dynamic I want to address is "the cost of free and good enough." The burning question is: What happens to push salespeople when technology becomes free and good enough? I asked a colleague of mine, Jeff Kane, what kept him up at night. His response was, "As the world changes, cheap and good enough is going to be cheap and good enough." He went on to add, "Let's say you're offering a product for $1,000. Here's a product with the same basic functionality that's free, or almost free via the 'Cloud.' Are you a thousand dollars better than free?"

Jeff brings up a good point. Not only is there a $1,000 dollar differential in this scenario, but there is also the cost of sourcing that salesperson. Your product is more expensive than the competition **and** your cost to market it is exponentially higher. As Jeff summed up, "If you want your business to survive in the 21st century, you better have an answer to that."

This becomes an issue to the push salesperson as well as the experienced advisor. The harsh reality is that as the push salesperson becomes extinct in this rapidly changing environment, the pull salesperson may be next on the endangered species list. Cheap and free is not a threat to one model of selling, it's a threat to all of selling.

In 2006, Wim Elfrink became Cisco's chief globalization officer. That same year he and his family, wife, kids and two dogs relocated to Bangalore, India. An interesting factoid about Bangalore is within a five-hour plane ride you can reach 70% of the world's population. That's important. So, Wim went to India with a specific purpose in mind. A lot of people will think it's because Cisco wanted to look into labor arbitrage in emerging markets. A lot of people would be wrong. That's why many companies would go there, but not Wim and not Cisco.

In 2006, Cisco did not have a true presence in the East. Wim went to India to set up what he called Cisco East. For Wim, creating a Cisco headquarters in India was all about talent, growth and innovation. *Talent* because India has over one billion people and graduates about 750,000 engineers per year[2]; *growth* because by 2020 two-thirds of the world's population is going to live in the East; and innovation because of the impact growth plus talent has on manufacturing, technology services and energy. Wim knew India would be a hotbed of innovation because that level of growth in the context of the Indian economic, political and social landscape would require and drive unique solutions.

---

[2] Kalpana, Pathak. "Engineering Graduates Could Become More 'Unemployable'" Business Standard. 02 June 2010. Web. 11 Nov. 2011. http://www.business-standard.com/india/news/engineering-graduates-could-become-more-unemployable/00/08/396771/.

During his tenure in India, Wim taught Cisco about "good enough" and innovative business models. At the time of writing, the average cellular revenue per user (ARPU) in India was around $6/month per user. The average revenue per user in the U.S. was approximately $55/month per user. Think about your own personal use between cable, Internet, cell phone, iPad, mobile data plans, and access to all the high-definition movies. Why the huge difference in ARPU between the U.S. and India? There are two primary reasons.

One reason is the U.S. usually has more bells and whistles in their products than they actually know how to use, or even need to use. This is called the "consumption gap." J.B. Wood, Todd Hewlin and Thomas Lah define the consumption gap in their book, *Consumption Economics: The New Rules of Tech*, as "the idea that technology companies can add features and complexity to their products at a much more rapid rate than their customers have the ability to consume them."[3]

The second reason is that in the U.S. there has not been an impetus from the market to drive costs down—at least not to a $6/month per user. The $55/month per user comes with an industry infrastructure and a business model that actually needs $55/month per user to support itself—not because fat corporations demand huge margins to feed the greed of their shareholders, but because the cost of doing business in the U.S. (taxes, labor, regulation, legal issues, etc.) is exponentially higher than India. There is also less of an appetite to innovate business models because of media and customer backlash in the U.S.

Here's India with an ARPU hovering around $6 while their telecom companies are still seeing an estimated 40% margin. And they still have more cell phones than they have cars. Contrary to what people may assume, the companies who are providing the technology in the "good enough" domain are making good profits. So the question is: How do businesses with high cost infrastructures, inefficient business models, and an underdeveloped ability to innovate compete against companies that do have these advantages? Looking at the solar industry, the answer is too often bankruptcy and closure.

---

[3] Wood, J. B., Hewlin, Todd, and Lah, Thomas. 2011. *Consumption Economics: The New Rules of Tech*. Point B Inc. (4)

Let's examine the consumption gap concept. Consider when General Electric wanted to market their latest and greatest medical diagnostics machine to India at a price tag of $100,000 per unit. To run it they needed highly skilled technicians with very specific training. Well, as it turns out India did not require all the features and functions. What it needed was a medical diagnostics machine that an average medical technician could use, and they needed it for about $15,000. So GE, like others, have had a difficult time going to market with products stuffed full of unneeded or unwanted functionality.

In the East, Wim and Cisco learned that the response to the demand for the "cost of free" is a functionally "cheap and good enough model" in which the consumption gap is tightened and customers get what they are actually looking for.

Now let's examine innovation. The truth is there are plenty of "bells and whistles" in products that India does want and need. This is not a matter of simply stripping out features and reducing the price, this is a "yes, and" matter—"**Yes,** there are some bells and whistles we need and want in our products **and,** we want the products at a price we can afford." In this case everything from product inception to development to manufacturing to supply chain to sales and marketing has to be good enough **and** inexpensive enough for that market. The true innovation here is in the business model, not necessarily the technology, or lack thereof. And that type of innovation can only come from a part of the world where, for example, there are over 600 million cell phone subscribers at $6/month per user. The scale is enormous!

There are two seemingly contradictory forces at play that meet in the middle. One is optimizing the consumption gap in favor of the customer. The second is developing innovative business models that can deliver quality products at a price sustainable by the market and at a margin a company can still thrive on.

Now let's go back to our "push" vs. "pull" conversation and let's broaden our thinking beyond just sales to include leadership. In an organization led by "push thinking," the customer would be in the background. The company would tell the customer what they wanted by providing one-size-fits-all products and services. The leaders of the company would look to their employees to fall in line, deliver against short-term goals and let the future take care of itself.

By contrast, an organization led by a "pull" type of mentality would put the customer as well as employees in the foreground, being open to the changing needs of the customer. The company would look to renovate its business model to provide solutions that satisfied the customer's immediate needs and even addressed their future needs. These solutions would come from staff empowered through teamwork-and-collaboration as opposed to command-and-control. Throughout the remainder of the book we will delve into how we make this seemingly idyllic vision a concrete reality.

 **INSTANT REPLAY**

Over the last several decades "push" has become the default mode of selling as a natural reaction to declining sales. To avert the decline we need to leverage pull selling. In this case, experienced advisors work to understand and meet customer needs. In leadership the same strategic agility is needed to get in front of where an organization needs to go and to help it, through its own innate talent, live up to its potential.

In leadership, just as in sales, there is push and pull. Leadership generally follows the nature of the product or service. Just as a salesperson in a push box must move a mountain to regain trust in their customer's eyes, so a leader must make monumental changes to get out of their own box. In the marketplace, stakeholders (employees, consumers, customers, shareholders) have more and more access to information and more and more access to choice.

Leaders who fail to make the transition to experienced advisors from command-and-control managers will become extinct. Their time-tested, proven push skills are perishable. Unfortunately they are liable to drag down entire companies in the process.

Atrophy affects leadership in the same way that it affects sales. The failure to exercise strong leadership skills built upon trust will result in the deterioration of those skills. In future chapters we will delve more into this area. Suffice it to say here that in comparison to sales skills gaps, leadership gaps reach deeper into an organization's foundations and lead to more devastating effects.

The leadership response to the "cost of free" and "good enough" challenge cannot be the responses noted in the Introduction—"cut headcount, sell assets, refocus back on their 'core,' master the supply chain." It also cannot be to strip out the functionality of products or the quality of services. To remain a viable business in the world of hyper-commoditization and "good enough and free," a company must keep the customer in the foreground and optimize their products and services to their needs. They must also develop innovative business models that can deliver those products and services at affordable price points and with margins strong enough to support an ongoing enterprise.

The market and cultural dynamics that are acting on business these days are formidable to say the least. What we have covered in this chapter is an in-depth view of what makes up those dynamics as well as some indicative responses. Most of this discussion, however, has been limited to sales. In the next section we'll take a closer look at leadership skills and how they can be an effective leverage against the immense pressures of today's competitive market.

What we have described in this chapter are three driving forces that all leaders are exposed to and succumb to at one time in their career. It is another cycle of insanity where managers and leaders react to the current environment and continue to rely upon time trusted and trained skills to do what they do best; solve the problems of today to build the future based upon the past.

Ask yourself these questions and write out your responses and discuss with a colleague:

- How have the Push and Pull sales models affected your management style and results?

- Who was your leadership role model and where have your leadership skills started to atrophy?

- How has the cost of free and just good enough affected how you manage or lead?

THE SCIENCE AND THE ART

"Winning is the best deodorant."

—JOHN MADDEN

CHAPTER THREE

THE SCIENTIFIC METHOD

We've examined some of the dynamics that have made up the leadership gap and have called out a leadership challenge. Now it's time to explore leadership skills. Let's take a look at the science of selling, which can be deeply analogous to the science of leadership. While it is not my intent to cover every aspect of selling, I will highlight primary aspects of the science of selling—calls, demos, practice and structure—to give a flavor for the rigor involved in the science of selling. And, as I noted in the introduction, since this book is only about the principles of sales insomuch as it allows us to create a parallel with leadership principles, we'll also explore the science of leadership, otherwise known as "management." Allow me first, however, to return to my story . . .

In the first three years of my sales career I worked on perfecting my sales methods. It wasn't long before I started making my territory numbers and then exceeding those numbers. True to the principle of "the harder you work, the luckier you get," I soon discovered I didn't actually need to work 40 hours to make my numbers. I could do it in less than 40. There was something about the consistent application of proven techniques that did the trick. Selling was indeed a science and the science was working.

So I had a choice. I could skate by on 30-40 hours a week doing just enough to make my numbers, or I could raise the bar. I decided to ratchet up my efforts to see what would happen. I put in more hours and practiced and honed my selling skills. The payoff was real and almost immediate. My monthly salary at the time was about $400, which in those days was decent money. My monthly commissions grew to $1,000 for the same time period. For a kid from the North side of Chicago that was more than decent money, that was *big* money.

I had the distinct pleasure those days of living at home with my parents while I put away some money to buy a car. Some days I'd spend the day with my manager being coached on the intricacies of sales only to go home and have dinner with my dad who would critique and coach me through the experiences again. It was like having two sales managers. I say this with appreciation. It was a wonderful opportunity to learn from the best, and I took advantage of that opportunity as much as I could.

A few weeks ago I saw a t-shirt that read, "I train while you sleep." I remembered my dad and recalled a lesson he taught me. He said, "Kid, most salespeople work a half day on Friday. I can tell you that every hour you work past noon on a Friday will pay off exponentially over the long run. The extra hours and extra effort you put in while others put on their hats and head home will translate to incremental sales within months." And he was right. I can say with hand on heart that his advice is as true now as it was all those years ago.

The increase in income was a huge incentive for me to put in the hours. The advice from my dad was another. The biggest incentive, however, was the thrill I felt when I set a goal and then accomplished it. In simple terms, "Boy, it felt good to win." Once I had the feeling I didn't want to let it go. I didn't want to be a winner for just one month, quarter or year. For me the proof was in building a track record of success. As any athlete will tell you, winning is one thing, continuing to win is another.

Determined to maintain my success, I tried to learn from every source available to me. I worked with a mentor, watched my managers and colleagues and listened avidly to my dad. I knew the only limit to my success would be how willing I was to spend the time and effort to improve.

CALLS + DEMOS = ORDERS

I learned the same classic sales techniques every salesperson learns: prospecting, qualifying, overcoming objections, proposing and closing. I quickly saw that if you can't proficiently step through the stages of the sales process, you won't get very far. Mastering these steps is essential to success in sales.

Any sales organization half serious about its business will make the science of selling a fundamental part of their training programs. I started my career in sales in the 1970s and today they still teach the same basics, though by different names. For example, "qualifying the prospect" has become "establishing rapport" and "understanding the business case."

The science of sales is no great hidden secret. It is made up of the tools and techniques that we can describe in a simple equation: Calls + Demos = Orders. The key to the science of selling is pushing volume through the calls + demos funnel. Enough calls will lead to a sizable amount of demos and a percentage of those demos will turn to orders. The trick is converting calls to demos and demos to orders. It's a numbers game.

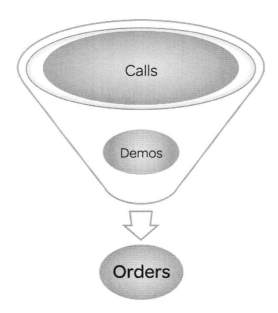

Again, the more things change, the more they stay the same. A colleague of mine, Mike Staver, says: "There once was a time when you could put your products in your bag, show up at your prospect's office and compete on features, benefits and price." Those times hearken back to the days of Willy Loman driving up and down the Eastern seaboard selling from the trunk of his car. Mike is quick to add, "That's not the case anymore."

Times are different. The optimization of the supply chain and advancing technology has radically changed the "vehicles" of selling—instead of selling out of sales bags with a smile and handshake, we now use email, text, teleconference, video conference, and other technologies to facilitate the sales process. How customers feel about salespeople has also changed. Instead of trusting salespeople's words, the public has learned to distrust salespeople and scrutinize them as "used cars salesman or marketing types." And finally, the cost of selling has also gone up. Let's explore these three nuances and the effect they have had on modern sales and, by extension, leadership.

- **Improved access to information:** Not only has technology changed how we approach selling from the seller's perspective, it has changed how customers approach the sales process as well. Technology has commoditized virtually all products by creating open access to the free and almost instant flow of information. Because customers have access to so much information about so many products, who carries them and the real costs, most sales have been stripped down to a transactional model.

The question of how technology changed leadership is about transparency. The expectation of open information doesn't end at the office door. What people experience in their daily lives, they also expect to experience in the workplace. In today's world, leaders have to learn to be forthcoming with their rationale behind decisions, they have to be clear about their strategic intentions and they have to be willing to have two-way communications.

- **Our reputation precedes us:** When sales managers demand an increase in the volume of prospects coming through the sales pipeline, many salespeople rely on the "wind shielding" technique. Wind shielding means the salesperson drives through their patch and literally takes visual note of prospective client's names on buildings and then adds them to their 90-day pipeline. Sometimes they may stop for a cold call, but more often they just follow up and prospect by phone. The idea is to drum up as many potential leads as possible to push through the calls + demos funnel.

"Drive-by selling" occurs when products are so much in demand they sell themselves. When a prospect calls for an appointment, the salesperson responds with a variation of, "I only have time for one sales call, so we can do the demo and then you can submit your order or we can take the order now and I can come do the installation." For many technology companies this was the hallmark of their Kool-Aid days in the late 90's.

A more figurative type of drive-by selling occurs *during* a sales call when a salesperson focuses only on getting a prospect to buy. They aren't interested in building true relationships, they aren't interested in problems the customer needs to solve, they aren't interested in objectives the customer needs to achieve; they are only interested in getting the customer to say "yes" and to sign the contract.

In leadership this type of mentality manifests itself in "leading by checklists" wherein a leader meets their leadership requirements by completing the requisite number of tasks mandated to them by human resources—e.g. have a career development discussion with each of your direct reports, complete an annual succession plan, complete an employee satisfaction survey. They perform these activities just enough to satisfy the minimum requirements before going out looking for more Kool-Aid!

- **Time is money:** Selling can be a labor intensive and therefore a costly process for the company—and for the customer since many of these costs are passed through. Simply put, selling in the traditional way requires both people and time: people to do the selling, and time to walk through all the steps of the sale. When you consider that this is a numbers game and that a certain percentage of sales prospects never progress beyond just being a prospect—well, you begin to get the idea that not all the time spent in sales equals the same result.

Now, this isn't just a sales problem. It's a leadership problem as well. In today's world where there is so much pressure for short term results, leaders analyze how they spend their time by commercial measures as opposed to intangible measures with returns that come in the way of employee and customer satisfaction and loyalty. Unfortunately, in this all too common scenario, customer and employee relations are put on the backburner for more transactional activities.

Now, let's put all these factors together: 1) Customers have more access to information and less need for salespeople; 2) Some salespeople have ruined it for the rest of us by abusing customer's trust creating a general dislike for salespeople; 3) Selling can be time consuming and costly.

Let's apply these terms to leadership. We can say 1) Employees expect more transparency from their leaders; 2) Some leaders have taken a checklist approach to leading and have thereby shirked their responsibility to their people and their customers; 3) Leading people can be time consuming and some leaders have opted to spend their time on other activities. What you have is a perfect storm for a leadership challenge, the perfect set up for the death of the leader.

THE CALL:
SOLVING THE CALCULUS OF PROBABILITY

A simple reminder—if a salesperson can sell the problem, the solution sells itself. The key to this is to understand your customer's problems. The point of the science in relation to a sales call is to anticipate your client's needs as well as their objections. Within the discrete steps of prospecting, qualifying, overcoming objections, proposing and closing are a ton of techniques and tactics all engineered, like a good offensive football play, to score a touchdown. The science of a sales call is about predicting reactions and formulating responses in order to strip out uncertainty and ensure winning a contract. The science of leadership encompasses many of the same approaches as the science of calls. A good sales manager will engineer processes, activities and human capital in the service of delivering objectives and mitigating risks to delivery. A manager is focused on delivering results by managing or supervising activities in the here and now. They are also focused on ensuring that no member of the team fails, as that would reflect directly upon them as managers.

As part of a sales call, a salesperson will conduct a thorough needs analysis. The purpose of a needs analysis is to assess the dynamics that are impacting a particular customer's business and ultimately affecting their ability to deliver against their objectives. The needs analysis usually begins before the initial sales call and continues as part of that first call, oftentimes extending into several calls, depending on the complexity of the account. During the needs analysis the salesperson typically does the following:

- Research the target company to understand their operating model, business plans and leverage points

- Discover who the relevant influencers are in the organization and determine a means to gain access to them

- Study and learn all the speeds/feeds and deliverables of the product or service they want to sell

- Conduct a competitive analysis to determine unique and distinctive selling points against potential competitors. (The interesting phenomenon is most salespeople only prepare and respond to the competition **after** they find out their potential client is considering them!)

- Identify potential objections the client may have and prepare answers to the objections

- Prepare a pitch based on the client's needs and the product's unique and distinctive selling points

- Calculate and prepare to present the client's potential return on investment (ROI)

In the science of leadership, formal needs analysis is normally tied to individual projects. A good manager, however, will have a deep understanding of operating models, business plans and objectives that are within their business or parts of other business units and functions that may impact them. They will also have a keen knowledge of the influencers who are positioned both laterally and above them. Lastly, they will know their internal and external competition inside and out.

The science of selling equips the salesperson with tools, like the needs analysis, necessary to engineer a call so that unique and distinctive selling points can be leveraged against the client's business needs in a way that is superior to the competition. The science of leadership is very similar. It encompasses careful planning with a thorough understanding of drivers and pressures that may impede or enhance the delivery of results. Altogether, whether in sales or leadership, the science is all about robust planning, selling value and delivering results.

THE DEMO: RHETORIC OF SIZZLE

Demos, as the name would suggest, are the opportunity for the salesperson to demonstrate what they can do for the customer. Demos are about showcasing **FABs—F**eatures of the product, **A**dvantages to the user and **B**enefits for the customer. Where physical products are involved, the salesperson will use actual demo units. Where services are involved, or when it isn't practical to demo an actual product, whiteboard presentations, videos and case studies are used.

Demo units have a rich and fun tradition in the sales world. You have to understand demo units aren't cheap knock offs of the products; they are the real McCoy. I have seen salespeople give their colleagues who were leaving for new jobs wonderful send offs replete with heartfelt farewell cards, touching mementos of the good old days and expensive, elaborate lunches. But before their best buddy can make it to their car, three or four former colleagues are in mortal combat over who can lay claim to the demo units left in the office.

Apart from the fun, the science of demos include engineering everything from the medium used to present the demo to scripting the conversation in advance. PowerPoint is a great way to combine the use of text with that of images or graphics. Videos are great for adding flair and pizzazz. Whiteboards and other non-permanent tools are great to highlight spontaneity and familiarity. As for scripting, well, as ironic as it may sound, the more a conversation is scripted and practiced—especially with stories of other customer successes—the more natural it will sound. The idea is to replace a formal, stilted tone with an extemporaneous, passionate story-like tone. As you can see, there isn't a whole lot of complexity to the science of a demo. It's a bit like show and tell.

The science of leadership, in parallel to demos, is also quite simple and relies largely on communication choices. Management's version of a demo is to communicate solely for the purpose of transmitting a technically correct message. This type of communication relies heavily on "broadcast" messaging—that is, messaging from a single source sent to a large audience with no opportunity for feedback or interaction. For instance, an email from a CEO to the entire organization is a broadcast message. Similarly a podcast from a CFO posted on the company intranet is also a broadcast message. The point is, the science version of leadership communications is all about one-way transmission. A riskier form of communication which would take place in the art of leadership is two-way communication. In two-way communication, leaders open themselves up to feedback and implicitly, if not explicitly, suggest they will act upon that feedback. Two-way communication tactics can be as simple as a Q&A session or as complicated as an ongoing blog.

PRACTICE (AND STRUCTURE) MAKES PERFECT

"You play like you practice," is as true in sales as it is in leadership, sports, and life. The principle is simple: The more you practice something, the easier it will become; and the more you integrate something into your personal way of working, the more sustainable it will become. Professional athletes practice four hours for every 15 minutes they "play."

> *"One time out loud is worth 10 times in your head."*
>
> —ED MUSSELWHITE, CEO, Mandel Communications, Inc.

Practice can be done on an individual and group basis. A salesperson can practice their pitch alone at home or in their office: talking out loud through the actual words they will say, working through the logical twists and turns, and becoming deeply familiar with responses to possible objections. Practice can also be done in front of audiences or a video camera—as in role playing during training. Group practice can be a special kind of torture that brings out the best and worst in people. There is something about having others in the room to watch, react and interact that adds that extra pressure, that brings you just a little closer to the intensity of a sales call.

Perfect practice enables perfect play, and imperfect practice leads to imperfect play. You can't just practice, you have to practice the right thing, or you burn in the wrong pattern.

The tool that helps to ease the tension of practice and reality is structure. Every salesperson will tell you they have their own particular style. Style is really nothing more than a structure founded on that salesperson's own experiences, refined through practice and reality, and accented by preference and personality. Most people develop a sales style or structure without even knowing it; it feels intuitive and natural. The fact is, you can improve anything you construct. Those who are open to continually practicing their sales structure tend to be more successful than those who see their structure as definitive and complete.

Part of any person's sales structure should be a set of killer questions. Questions are the tool used to understand your client's business needs, objectives and challenges from their perspective. No amount of desktop research will produce the same insights as posing thoughtful open-ended questions to a client. Now, when we think of a set of killer questions, it screams "Science." The trick is that while a set of questions may feel formulaic, what they generate and how that is used is very much art-based.

At one point in my career with Cisco I created a tool called Customer Support Requirements Analysis (CSRA). CSRA was comprised of 130 questions that enabled a salesperson to enter into a Socratic dialogue with their clients. The tool helped salespeople to understand which questions to ask depending on their particular situation. It also helped them walk through the analysis process. The tool, however, was not meant as a traditional training tool—that is, I wasn't going to hand the tool to our training team and ask them to build a program around it. It would have been as painful as a root canal for both trainer and participant. Instead I expected them to use the tool as a guide. Once the salesperson understood how to use the tool, once they understood what the questions really asked and what the responses really meant, the tool was no longer needed. The tool was a short cut to experience.

Anyone who has taught a teenager how to drive can relate to this model. If we do a quick online search for "steps for using turn signals," we will find the average number of steps is five. Five steps to flick on a turn signal. Now, think of all the other things you have to know to drive and add up the steps in total. Now, think of the average attention span of the average teenager. *Scary.* What we do with teenage drivers is give them all those steps and hope that through practice they can develop their driving structure in such a way that prevents them from causing any harm to people or property.

The CRSA tool I developed for my transactional sales staff was meant to accelerate the science lifecycle and move forward the consultative learning curve. In short, it provided structure that would augment their ability to learn from their experiences. For me, that was the beginning of creating a sales system, but more on that later.

> *"The science has to do with the technical elements, mostly features, benefits, and price, quality of product, competitive analysis, marketplace functionality, that kind of thing. The art is not only the charisma with which the sales professional works, but the level of emotional intelligence. More importantly, a sales professional has to be able to effectively diagnose what their perspective customer needs in real time all the time."*
>
> —MIKE STAVER, CEO, The Staver Group

UNVEILING THE ART

Let me be clear. As disingenuous as the science of selling may sound, it is absolutely foundational to the next and higher level of selling as well as leadership, a level I call "the art." Without mastering the science, a salesperson can never hope to progress to the art. And without progressing to the art, a salesperson and a leader will go the way of Willy Loman.

So what does the art of selling look like in comparison with the science? Let's use demos to take an early look.

The science of demos is about showing off the FAB's of your product or service, but the art of demos is much more. The art of demos is about listening and communication—not one-way communication but two-way dialogue. During a demo the salesperson has the opportunity to recap what they have learned about the prospect's case, playing back what they understand to be the internal and external pressures and drivers impacting the potential client. A demo doesn't necessarily have to pinpoint all the right information and decisions at the moment; in fact, some of the most successful demos are ones in which the client offers up more clarifying information to help fine tune the solution. Where the science prescribes techniques and tools to walk through this information to best keep the prospect's attention, the art allows for agreement on what problems need to be and provides adequate "check in" time to ensure the client's particular situation is captured correctly and that there is concurrence. If there is concurrence, then the customer may be compelled to purchase not only in the short-term but they are likely to make repeat orders as long as a customer focused relationship is maintained.

We have all heard of or, if we are lucky, worked for leaders who we would follow into hell and back. We don't follow a leader into hell and back because they transmit good information, we do it because we have a connection to them founded on trust—in other words, a relationship.

The ultimate goal of a science-based demo is to demonstrate FABs in such a compelling way that an order is secured. The ultimate goal of an art-based demo is to demonstrate deep understanding of the customer's business objectives, express genuine desire to help meet those objectives and instill conviction that you can provide the solution needed. The end result may be repeated orders, or it may be a concession that you cannot provide the necessary solution based on the customer's real needs. Either way, as you begin to build a relationship with the customer through active listening and earnestly trying to meet their needs, you gain the customer's respect. The differentiator, then, between the science and the art is relationships.

If we consider the equation we started with in the beginning of this chapter which articulates the science of selling as:

Calls + Demos = Orders

If we were to similarly script an equation for the art of selling based on our limited discussion, we come up with the following:

(Calls + Demos) / Relationships = Repeated Orders

The nuance of relationship is the distinguishing factor that lifts a call and a demo from the science to the art. For example, it is not presentation of material that differentiates a demo, but the ability of the salesperson to listen to the customer, reach concurrence through a common understanding and develop trust. In the needs analysis aspect of a sales call it is the deep understanding of the customer's world that distinguishes it from the science. In all cases, the art is founded in relationships.

Our understanding of both the science and art of leadership will evolve as we progress through the chapters that follow. If we build out a corollary equation for the science and art of leadership as we understand them at the moment, we have:

- **Science of leadership:** Planning + Communication = Management
- **Art of leadership:** Strategy + Communication / Relationships = Leadership

Just as with the science and art of sales, in the science and art of leadership one's ability to build a relationship is the differentiating denominator. Our equations, of course, are crude representations and fail to capture the richness of either management or leadership. I would also say that as we compare relationships to planning and communication, those features change dramatically. For instance, when planning is vetted through relationships—e.g. when we integrate relationships with planning and communication—the situation changes dramatically. For instance, when a plan is validated through a relationship you get back far more than a simplistic check of steps and sequence. You also learn what is strategically important to the various stakeholders involved.

Relationships are based on a delicate balance of communicating and connecting, especially in a world where collaboration is becoming more and more important.

I have found that clarity, timing, and alignment drive effective communications.

- **Clarity:** Clarity underpinned by correctness and cohesiveness (the three big Cs) are king in communications. You won't move the needle very far if people don't understand the message, if the message is incorrect and if it is inconsistent with other messages you have conveyed.

- **Timing:** Timing is a huge part of the message itself. *The right message at the wrong time is the wrong message.*

- **Alignment:** How we deliver our message must be aligned with the intent of our message. For instance, a quavering voice will not effectively convey a message about confidence.

In addition, connections are created and strengthened by being present, vulnerable and receptive.

- **Presence:** Being present with your audience—be it an audience of one or 1,000—initiates a connection. Just because you are in the room doesn't mean that you are actually there. Being present means listening, absorbing and reflecting.

- **Vulnerability:** By allowing yourself to be vulnerable you improve the stickiness of connections. Being vulnerable does not mean being weak and weepy, it means showing that you are open about who you are; you are not afraid to take criticism and you are willing to change.

- **Receptive:** Listening to others without threat of judgment and allowing others the possibility of influencing decisions is the mark of being receptive. Listening without the possibility of acting upon what is said is simply hearing.

 **INSTANT REPLAY**

The goal of the science of a sales call is to maximize the possibility of securing an order. This may or may not be in the best interest of the potential client. The science of a sales call is completely oriented toward the closing of the sale, the signing of an order.

The art of a sales call follows much the same methodology as the science, but is focused on benefiting the customer. This means that based on the business objectives of a client, a salesperson may need to concede that they do not have the best solution or that their solution may not exactly match the needs of the client. The risk, of course, is the possibility of losing the order. The art of a call yields different results from the science of a call; this difference suggests that solely focusing on a short-term win benefits the salesperson's firm and may ultimately damage the reputation of the salesperson's firm by eroding their perceived value by the customer.

A large part of the science of leadership is about formulating actions based on the near-term dynamics of a market and immediate conditions of the organization. In short, the science of leadership is about planning and managing tactics in service of short- or near-term results. The science of leadership is better known as management. As with the science of a call, there are aspects of the science of leadership which are absolutely essential to the health of an enterprise. In addition, as in sales, one should not expect to progress to the art of leadership without first mastering the science.

Practice and structure are principles that help embed the science and art of both selling and leadership. You play and sell and lead like you practice. Practice is generally done on an individual basis, while group practice adds the pressure of having a live audience and better approximates real-world pressures. Structure is akin to style. The key is that structure can be improved by conscious and formal effort. As we improve our structure and then run it through practice it becomes a natural part of our repertoire. Practice and structure applied to the science of sales and leadership with the added sauce of relationship will, over time, help one cross over to the art.

The art of leadership takes the principles of communication and combines them with the power of relationships. So, in the science of leadership, a manager clearly conveys his or her plans and expectations about the implementation of tactics through the proper communication channels to the proper people at the proper time. In the art of leadership, the leader conveys messages about the vision and strategy through the proper communication channels to the proper people at the proper time, and they do it in such a way as to build engagement and commitment.

CHAPTER FOUR

THE ARTISTIC ENDEAVOR

Let's dive deeper into the art of selling and the art of leadership. If the science of selling is about engineering the risk out of sales by mastering key technical skills, then the art of selling is about creating connections with customers based on the needs of the customer and not on a need to sell your product. It is about building relationships through trust, instilled by demonstrating an authentic desire to help the client achieve their business objectives. The art of selling is also about acumen and agility—knowing your industry so well that you can teach your clients insights, possibilities and limitations. It's about becoming an experienced advisor. The ultimate goal is to instill conviction that you can provide the solutions they need.

If we step back and consider leadership, the same principles apply. The science of leadership is actually management. Management is focused on delivering activities and milestones in service of strategic objectives. While management is tactical in nature and is about mitigating risks and driving day-to-day performance, leadership is strategic in nature and is about galvanizing an organization toward a long-term vision.

For me nothing illustrates theory better than a story. In the following pages I'll cover some theoretical perspectives about the art of selling, and by analogy the art of leadership, and then show how they came to life in my experiences and those of my colleagues.

MIRROR, MIRROR

If we go back to our equation of Calls + Demos = Orders, there is an ideal ratio of calls to demos. Once a salesperson has mastered the sales call, they will reach a stable conversion ratio of turning those calls into demos and then turning those demos into orders. The better you are at sales calls, the more demos you will create; the better you are at demos, the more orders you will generate. But there is a limit to that conversion ratio, so eventually the only way to increase orders is by increasing the volume of the pipeline. If you want more stuff to come out of the bottom of the funnel, you have to pour more in the top.

Over time the only way to increase the orders generated is by opening or expanding into a new market, introducing new products, and/or changing your sales or coverage model. Or, you can move into the art of selling, which increases your conversion rate by improving the efficiency of the sales process and enhancing customer loyalty through stronger relationships founded on the trust model. You can't achieve the same levels of efficiency and customer service through the science of selling. It's hard to create a healthy sales relationship with transactional drive-by selling or shaking hands over the Internet.

> *In a research study conducted at Cisco in 2005, it was discovered for every 1% increase in customer loyalty there was an approximate $20M boost lifetime in sales for a large enterprise customer. A decrease in customer loyalty, it was found, had the reverse effect.*

A helpful way to understand how the science relates to the art is to think of a two-way mirror. You only see a reflection of your own interests. When you are steeped in the science of selling (and leadership), your only interests are your own. Your vision is limited to your side of the mirror. When you are steeped in the art of selling (and leadership), you understand there are two sides to every mirror and need to see both your own interests and the customers. This allows you deliver a solution to satisfy both.

When a salesperson is on the science side of the mirror, they do everything in a systematic effort to land an order. Their efforts, through instruction or experience, become a prescribed methodology focused on one outcome: the order. When the salesperson starts doing things from the customer's perspective, they see through to the other side of the mirror. From this perspective they still work for the order, but they do it as an experienced advisor, as someone who is genuinely interested in seeing the customer succeed.

Staying on the customer side of the mirror—the art side—takes a lot of effort. And if there is one thing people dislike, it's having to expend a lot of extra effort or changing their behavior. I'm not saying people are inherently lazy, but I am saying human nature will opt for the path of least resistance. If there are 25 steps a salesperson has to walk through to make an order, and they realize they can reduce the process by 10 steps and still make an order, that new 15-step process will become the favored method. With that in mind, once they can see the art side of the mirror there is the real danger that the activity that enabled the salesperson to get there will become a temporary step in their methodology of closing a deal. At that point they are right back to the science side. If we reference our earlier model, this behavior would describe a talented, transactional vendor. Relationship building cannot just be a step **in the process** to closing a deal; it has to **be the process.**

Customers know which side of the mirror their salesperson resides on. Anyone in sales who has never validated how they are perceived by their customer may be surprised at their customer's response.

ITALIAN RESTAURANT

I recall when I first became aware that there were two sides of the mirror and that maybe I was on the wrong side. I learned that by building a relationship you do not give up your ability to close the order; rather, you create the opportunity for repeat orders.

Business dinners are a rite of passage in the sales world. Whether they are networking opportunities within your company or a dinner with clients, every person in sales is bound to become a business dinner veteran. I recall my first business dinner with a client. I was a young salesperson, still at A.B. Dick. My manager arranged a dinner with a potential client at a nice Italian restaurant just outside the Chicago loop. The name of the restaurant was the Como Inn and I have perfect recall of what we ordered (gnocchi with a pesto cream sauce and side of sausage) and what I learned that night (the importance of relationships).

We met our clients at the restaurant and after the perfunctory hellos, handshakes, and small talk we took our drinks to our seats and ordered dinner. I remember flipping through the menu in a buzz. Who cared what we were going eat? I remember feeling exasperated as everyone chatted about what looked good and what wine would go with what entrée. All I wanted to talk about was which of our products best suited their needs and how many they should order! For me, food and drinks and conversation were a distraction to what we were there for.

> *"The art is the ability to build effective relationships with prospective and existing clients. And that's done really through effective interpersonal skills. There's a certain degree of personality, but true art requires dogged determination. It requires energy, enthusiasm, team spirit and a variety of other attributes and qualities that are extremely important."*
>
> —JERE BROWN, CEO, Americas, Dimension Data

Dinner progressed like a slow motion opera for me. As the bread and then starters and entrée and finally deserts and after-dinner drinks came and went, so did the opportunities to land the deal. I kept bringing the conversation back to the business, but my manager kept thwarting my efforts by going off on tangents about vacation spots, bucket lists, personal anecdotes, social and family stuff. The clients were more than happy to oblige. Although the conversation was lively and animated, I was increasingly frustrated that we weren't getting down to business. I felt like I was in a silent wrestling match with my mentor, and I was losing. I kept looking for the signals and finally just let him lead us in what I saw as the obviously wrong direction. I remember feeling disappointed in myself and in my manager—I began to wonder if my manager was all he was cracked up to be.

After dinner we shook hands with the prospect and headed back to our car. Standing in the parking lot, my manager turned to me and said in a kind but direct voice, "George, you probably thought that we were here to close the deal. Wrong. We came here to have dinner. *Relationships first, business second.*"

I felt like a kid standing in front of one of my football coaches, head bowed and humbled, slowly realizing just how mistaken I had been. This is why we have sales leaders, I thought, because all those textbooks, professors and coaches, as great as they are, can't cover everything. Any sales trainer can teach you about the functionality of a product, enough time analyzing data can give you the leverage points of a company, but it takes an experienced guide to show you how to adjust your behaviors in a meaningful way. Learning how to build trust, how to build a relationship is an art.

 To learn an art you need the right artist to teach you.

CHALLENGE STRENGTHENS RELATIONSHIPS

I doubt if there is a sales training program or sales book today that fails to cover relationship building as a means to securing sales. The key is the *quality* of relationship. In a recently published study by Matthew Dixon and Brent Adamson, the authors describe one type of salesperson as the "relationship builder." They describe the relationship builder as focusing "on developing strong personal and professional relationships and advocates across the customer organization. They are generous with their time; strive to meet customers' every need, and work hard to resolve tensions in the commercial relationship."[4] On the surface, this description is generic enough to fit well within the parameters of the art of selling. However, as the writers define this type of salesperson further, they add that relationship builders "focus on relieving tension by giving

---

[4] Dixon, Matthew, and Brent Adamson. "Selling Is Not About Relationships." HBR Blog Network - Harvard Business Review. Web. 15 Oct. 2011. http://blogs.hbr.org/cs/2011/09/selling_is_not_about_relatio.html.

in to the customer's every demand." In my estimation, and that of Dixon and Adamson, this type of relationship builder is not what you would expect from a salesperson practicing the art of selling. In fact, it is more in line with how the art might look like practiced by someone who cannot move beyond the science of selling.

Dixon and Adamson then describe a salesperson type they call a "challenger." "Challengers use their deep understanding of their customers' business to push their thinking and take control of the sales conversation. They're not afraid to share even potentially controversial views and are assertive—with both their customers and bosses." This type of salesperson, according to their studies, outperforms all others. I think this is helpful, but imperfect. For me a good salesperson practicing the art of selling **builds relationships through healthy challenge.** With this context, I describe relationship building in the art of selling as follows:

- Being **vested** in the customer's business objectives and demonstrating a real interest in their personal and professional success

- Having the **integrity** to say "I don't know" and "no," and providing transparency into you and your company's actual capabilities

- Knowing your industry so well that you can **teach** your clients insights. In other words, get in front of where they are going and offer new possibilities

Healthy relationships in selling and leadership are predicated on healthy challenge. Without the challenge, the relationship is hardly worth the effort.

THE BEST OF THE WORST

After I had been with Cisco for a few months, I was asked to attend a sales call at a large insurance provider. I was warned the customer was unhappy with some of our services and prices. "Great," I thought, "they think we're not delivering and we cost too much. What a way to start a relationship!"

I joined two of my team in a large conference room on the third floor of the client's office. There were 12 or so members of their information technology staff and three of us. We were definitely feeling outnumbered.

In walked the lead for the insurance firm like a somber Brahma bull. We'll call him Bill for the convenience of this story. Bill strolled up to the head of the table and glanced down both sides where my team and I were spread out amongst his team. We made short introductions and then he looked at me and without a smile began:

"George," he said, "it's very nice to have you come to see us today, but I've got to tell you a few things. The first thing is . . . ." He then rolled into a litany of our sins from an inability to deliver, to an inability to deliver on time, to an inability to deliver on budget. He went on for a good ten minutes, summing up by saying, "The only thing I can tell you is that all the other vendors are no good, but you, Cisco, you suck the least."

So we were the best of the worst; at least I had a starting point.

The room went silent. I knew this was going to be one of those defining moments. I have learned from a long history of intense moments that a calm demeanor helps disarm almost any situation. I leaned forward in my chair and said, "Bill, thank you very much for sharing. If I can, I'd just like to ask you a few questions to get a few more details so that eventually, as we work together I can reestablish Cisco's credibility with you."

I realized that not only did we need to do a better job of delivering high quality service to him, but we needed a shared definition of success. I asked him a series of questions, although I knew at that point what the answers would be:

- How often do we talk to you about your company's business objectives, about where you are going over the next one to three years?

- How well do our teams get along together?

- Have we agreed upon the accountabilities for my team and for your team?

- Have we agreed what success is for your organization?

- If something goes wrong, do we have a defined escalation path?

- Finally, do we have a common set of metrics in place?

The answer to all the questions was "no," as I knew it would be. I looked at my team and nodded. We had a clear way forward. There were four indices we had to focus on:

- A common definition of success and a means to track it

- A way to measure the quality of communication at all the significant touch points between our client and us

- Clear roles, responsibilities and agreed upon metrics with accountabilities

- A defined escalation path that actually worked

By the way, these are four indices every service provider should track with their clients (internal and external). It comes down to a commitment to cadence and quality—regularly scheduled time for deep, open discussions (otherwise known as Level 2 discussions, which we will cover later). Proactive, meaningful communications will keep you ahead of the bus; reactive, rote communications will place you under the bus.

It is one to thing find yourself under the bus from time to time—we all make mistakes, and mistakes can be a good thing since that's how we learn—however, if you keep making the same mistake, it's like having the bus back up and move forward, over and over again. Not learning from your mistakes is painful.

The point of this story is, I had a wealth of experience to pull from to help me manage the call. I had an idea of the basic scenario—unhappy with our service, thinks we cost too much—so I immediately began to think through similar situations I had experienced. In fact, two weeks before a customer had taken me "out to the woodshed" on a few of the exact same points. Being a quick learner, as we discussed Bill's issues in more detail, I started to suggest processes tied to metrics that would mutually improve the situation. The solution we agreed on wasn't something I made up on the spur of the moment. It was based on principles I had seen proven out many times before; the same principles which I had recently experienced.

Being able to draw from experience is one thing, being able to present that information in a credible and cohesive way is another. If you want to be able to build relationships by drawing on your experience you'll need more than luck on your side. Simply said, "dive and catch" saves feel great, yield results and allow you to play hero for a day, but over the long run they're not sustainable. A great game comes down to practice and structure.

The team that had previously worked with Bill was not incompetent. In point of fact, they were quite well versed in their area of expertise. The problem was that area of expertise was limited to the science of selling. The skill I brought to the table, literally on that day, was that I took the customer's perspective and created a collaborative atmosphere in which we could build a solution that directly addressed the customer's needs. Part of what I did was science—e.g. four indices, a scorecard and methodology—and part of what I did was art—drawing from extensive experience and applying lessons learned to the situation at hand. The beauty of this event was in its recursive nature. I drew from a wide breadth of experiences to work through an immediate problem. My team, who had been stuck at this juncture, learned from the situation and then added it to their repertoire of experiences. Two things became part of their toolkit that day: A relationship dashboard we created with the client and the art of "experience mining."

To this day the account team still talks about that meeting as being the most pivotal moment in our relationship with Bill and his company. In the months that followed, my team and I delivered on everything we promised and more. We met our metrics (and in some cases over-delivered), gained his trust and rebuilt our credibility. Those months of strong delivery turned to years of unsurpassed service. That one meeting began to lay the foundation of a long-term business relationship between that account and Cisco and a long-term personal friendship with Bill. I have been great friends with Bill and his wife for over 12 years now.

THE VALUE OF "I DON'T KNOW"

A key to the art of both selling and leadership is not rushing in with prescribed solutions that only revolve around your interests. In sales this manifests itself when you try to sell your product regardless of the customer's needs; in services it plays out when promises are made without fully appreciating or defining the problem; in leadership it happens when leaders force feed their organization solutions without soliciting input. A better way forward is to pose the situation or context and then allow the customer or employees to fill in the blanks—that is, you allow them to tell you what their problem or solution might be.

A simple example of not filling in the blanks so quickly is a sales 101 technique called the "pregnant pause." When a customer asks a question that you can answer in five seconds flat, it is better to pause, reflect and even ask a reframing question before providing the answer. The science would have you answer the question in five seconds, like a gunslinger shooting bottles off the top of a fence. If you wait a few seconds before you answer, and I mean genuinely pause instead of immediately answering the question, it sends a message back that you care about the question or concern. You build empathy that you have listened and demonstrate that you value the question as well as the person who asked it. It shows you care enough to want to get it right.

This is counterintuitive to what the science (of selling as well as leadership) teaches us about anticipating the needs and pre-fitting your solution to those projected needs. In the art, you accept that you do not have all the answers and, indeed, that your customers or employees have a huge part to play in determining the solution. You open yourself up to the risk that the solution may be outside of your company's ability (in the context of sales) or your personal comfort zone (in the context of leadership). In this respect, the art is a more risky route to take. When you pass the proverbial pen to the customer or employees you are relinquishing some aspect of control. When you relinquish control, your ability to manage the outcome is compromised. Handing over control even for a short time can be a very scary thing, especially for a leader. For many leaders, control is the ultimate power. True power, however, is the ability to lead by allowing others a voice. The paradox in the art is that sometimes in order for the team to win you have to give up the ball.

I asked my colleague Jeff Kane to share the story of his first successful sale. He thought for moment and then said, "You know, I can only think of my first sales failures."

"That's interesting," I thought. And it is. The way we define failure has been crafted by a society that says clear and overt winning is the only acceptable definition of success. The reality is losing is often the first step to winning. As my head coach at Northern Illinois University, Jerry Ippoliti, often says, "We didn't lose, we just ran out of time."

I recast my question to Jeff. "Tell me the story of your first sale." He told the following story which for me speaks to the genesis of the difference between the science of selling and the art of selling. Look for the instances where Jeff followed the traditional science of selling and where he deviated. It is in the deviation where the art of selling emerges.

Back in the late 1990s I had started with one of the big five consulting firms. A friend of mine tipped me to a prospect that may be in the market to build a worldwide ATM network.

I said, "Sounds good, but what's ATM?" I figured it wasn't an automated teller machine network because it was a government organization not a bank. Now, this was before the power of Google but still in the Internet days. I went through my not so reliable dial-up, pay-by-minute Internet service and began my research. Indeed, I found out it meant "asynchronous transfer mode." I studied everything about ATMs I could find, which wasn't a lot. Still, I found books, I hunted down white papers, and I read and I read.

Finally, I ventured a cold call to the customer. "I understand you're working on an ATM project," I said.

The gentleman responded, "Yes, we are. Can you be here tomorrow? I'll clear a couple of hours."

This was not the introduction I was expecting, but it was first of many surprises to come. I may not have known a lot about asynchronous transfer modality, but I knew enough not to balk in the face of good fortune. The next day I arrived at their offices brimming with ATM knowledge and too much caffeine. The information I had dug up on ATMs was paltry, so I was mostly relying on the caffeine.

The gentleman I was meeting said a few more people would be joining us, including the agency Chief Information Officer. "Oh, good," I said, feeling cold sweat begin to roll down my back. There I was, a brand new salesperson armed with coffee induced confidence and just enough information to make me dangerous. I was bracing for the moment when they would ask me to leave.

The CIO came in and introduced himself. He was a nice enough fellow. He shook my hand and told me they were really looking for help with their project. I nodded and said, "Great." The gentleman whom I presumed was leading the project began talking in sweeping generalities about what they were trying to accomplish, what they were up against, the history of the agency and on and on. What he didn't say was what the project was. After some time he paused and asked me if I had any questions.

"Yes," I said, feeling nervous because I knew despite my better judgment I was about to ask something really stupid and potentially disastrous. "What is this project actually about?"

There was an awkward pause. My stomach fell. I thought it was probably time to say, "Thank you," gather my things, and leave. Then the project lead started to laugh; typically not a good sign.

He explained the project was to integrate a hodgepodge of systems and technologies into one cohesive enterprise system. The first step was to build a financial and technical business case. He wanted to work through that immediately, so we spent the next three hours white-boarding ideas. When we were done I said, "Sir, this has been a fantastic first meeting. I can't thank you enough for the education as well as your time. When should I follow up?"

He looked at me and asked, "Can we have your proposal by Friday so we can kick this project off?"

And so we started the project with a $120,000 order. By the end of the first year we had sold and delivered $17-million of projects to this customer.

Spring forward several years: I was getting ready to leave the firm for a better opportunity. Before I left I went back to the customer and let him know. We talked about who would be handling the agency's account and shared contact information for future networking. I had to ask him why it was he chose us so many years before. We certainly couldn't have presented the best case, and I know we weren't the cheapest bid.

His response surprised me. He said out of all the consultants and experts who had come to talk to them, I was the only person who had the courage to ask what the heck they were talking about. He explained, "I had five companies all saying 'yes' and not one of them knew what the project even entailed. I figured if you had the courage to ask, you would have the courage to stop us from doing something stupid."

Sometimes ignorance is a good thing.

For me, Jeff's story is a perfect example of what the science of selling teaches our salespeople never to do. "Never put a prospective deal at risk by asking stupid questions." The science of selling would say not having all the answers is a bad thing, that ignorance is a vacuum best filled with research on the seller's behalf. The art of selling would say, asking the customer to fill in the blanks will actually lead to a better solution. As my dad always told me, "Kid, selling is simply asking great questions." I would later add *even stupid ones.*

What Jeff did was brilliant, though he didn't know it at the time. First he followed the science to best of his ability. He followed up on an obscure lead, did his research, made that cold call and braved his way into a meeting with a customer who at the time was only a prospect. On the art side, he showed up as himself and followed his gut, which was to have the integrity to point out the proverbial elephant in the room. Jeff was willing to risk failure in order to succeed. His motivation was to protect the interests of the customer. He needed to know what the project was about before he could commit to completing it. The customer recognized this as a valued trait and the rest is history.

To this day, Jeff still corresponds with that client. He feels the biggest value from that interaction wasn't the $17-million in sales, but the lesson he learned. Simply put, while a salesperson can engineer their way into a sale, repeat orders come through relationships and trust, and trust is built on transparency. Another great lesson my father taught me was, "Kid, in selling and in life, relationships trump talent all day long."

When you ask a question that reveals your vulnerability, it shows that you can be trusted. And while trust is not the totality of a relationship, it is the beginning of a relationship.

From what Jeff first thought was a disastrous call, emerged a lesson about the art which can be applied to selling, leadership and life he would never forget. He followed his instincts and asked a risky question. That one question became part of the art he was to practice thereafter. By revealing that he didn't have all the answers, he demonstrated he was open to ideas other than his own, that he was honest about his current knowledge set, and, finally, that he needed input from others to build the right solution. How many leaders would be willing to make such an admission? How many leaders, when faced with a dilemma, would rather do it their way rather than ask for help from the organization? As a leader, what would you do?

THE HIGHEST CALLING

The ability to teach customers and provide insights only comes with accumulation of years of experience. I like to say once you have your BS in the science of selling and once you have your MBA in the art of selling, you begin to enter the space where you have the presence of mind, agility of wits, composure and acumen to begin to teach your customers. In the art of selling you should always have the ability to teach and the openness to be taught.

During my tenure with Amdahl we had a large bank client that needed to replace their Portfolio Information Management System (PIMS). The replacement project was one of the largest, and most complex that they'd ever undertaken. Their concerns were understandable as their existing mission critical platform was nearing end-of-life. Had I been operating from the science side of the mirror, I would have cashed in the order and let them deal with the pain of implementation. Instead, I took another tack which was rooted directly in the art side of the mirror.

In the PIMS project there were two basic aspects of the system—the application software and the platform (hardware, operating software and database). Anyone who has been part of a systems changeover can attest to how much time, labor and resources—human capital—is required for a successful outcome.

We scoped the project and decided to include a proof of concept. We did this on Amdahl's dime, as a service to the customer to help them better understand the intricacies of the project. Having been through several similar projects, I suspected that we could change the platform from an IBM mainframe to Sun Solaris with little downtime for the overall system, minimal impact to the users and considerably less cost and pain to the client. Our proof of concept showed just that.

We sat down with the customer and walked them through our findings. There was true excitement in the room when they saw we would be able to switch out their legacy platform earlier than anticipated, with a very strong return on investment and the required stability. What I was able to teach them was that the key to unlocking value in an enterprise system is in the application and not the platform. Understanding this and appreciating our customer's pain points, we were able to get in front of the headlights and arrive where they were going before they did. We invested our time and our money in an end-to-end solution path that we knew would be right based on their needs. Once they saw this, we had a long-term customer as opposed to a short-term deal.

When we consider the idea of an experienced advisor, whether it be in terms of sales, leadership or life, the value of that experience comes in sharing. Leaders will fail to lead if they hoard their wisdom to themselves and only apply it when it benefits them.

DELIBERATE PRACTICE

It wasn't until I had many years of sales under my belt—ten years of deliberate practice as K. Anders Ericsson would say[5]—that I stepped over to the art side of the mirror and was able to take on the customer's perspective. I learned that to be a successful salesperson I needed to master the science of selling, but to sustain that success I needed to master the art. An important point is that as you transcend to the art side of the mirror, the science doesn't go away. The science is necessary; the science is good. It becomes bad when that's all there is, when the art is left out of the equation or when the art is used in service of the science. The science is foundational but incomplete. The science is also easily replicated by the competition. The art, on the other hand, is not so easily replicated.

The other nuance, of course, is to focus on the customer outcome. The science generally yields short-term results. This is not to say that the art cannot be

---

[5] "Many characteristics once believed to reflect innate talent are actually the result of intense practice extended for a minimum of 10 years." Ericsson, K. Anders. 1993. "The Role of Deliberate Practice in the Acquisition of Expert Performance". Psychological Review. 100 (3): 363-406.

> *"I see some salespeople that just can't strike the human relation piece of it. There's that interpersonal skill and mapping that is so important to sales because, by the way, I don't think you really 'sell.' I think you inform and solve. Some of the best salespeople I've ever seen are coaches and teachers."*
>
> —WOODY SESSOMS, SVP, Global Enterprise, Cisco Systems

short-term-based. Relationships, after all, need to be maintained. As more of the art enters a sales relationship the outcome begins to morph. Those repeated orders transform into customer loyalty. Customer loyalty has several advantages over single transactions. First, customer loyalty is enduring. Second, customer loyalty is forgiving. Our equation now reads:

(Calls + Demos) / Relationships ★ 10,000 Hours = Customer Loyalty

At the end of those three years at A.B. Dick, I had to master the equation above in order to sustain my success. Of course, I didn't have that equation written out anywhere. It was a sense (role-modeled by my father), an intuition, an understanding that just following prescribed steps was not enough to keep me ahead of the curve. Over the next several years I learned that the art of sales is a deceptively simple concept. Once learned, however, its application expands far beyond the world of sales and into leadership.

Malcolm Gladwell says it takes about 10 years, or 10,000 hours, of practice to attain true expertise.

"The people at the very top don't just work harder or even much harder than everyone else," Gladwell writes. "They work much, much harder. Achievement," he says, "is talent plus preparation." Preparation seems to play a bigger role.

For example, he describes the Beatles: They had been together seven years before their famous arrival in America. They spent a lot of time playing in strip clubs in Hamburg, Germany, sometimes for as long as eight hours a night. Overnight sensation? Not exactly. Estimates are the band performed 1,200 times before their big success in 1964. By comparison, most bands don't perform 1,200 times in their careers.

Neurologist Daniel Levitin has studied the formula for success extensively and shares this finding: "The emerging picture from such studies is that 10,000 hours of practice is required to achieve the level of mastery associated with being a world-class expert in anything. In study after study of composers, basketball players, fiction writers, ice skaters, concert pianists, chess players, master criminals and what have you, the number comes up again and again. Of course, this doesn't address why some people get more out of their practice sessions than others do. But no one has yet found a case in which true world-class expertise was accomplished in less time. It seems it takes the brain this long to assimilate all that it needs to know to achieve true mastery." As Malcom Gladwell puts it, "Practice isn't the thing you do once you're good. It's the thing you do that makes you good."

In one sense, the science of selling and leadership can be easily mastered. The science is ruled by prescribed steps, processes and procedures. The art, however, is much more difficult because it is much more variable. The art hinges on relationships, and relationships are built around and with other people. No matter how much of a "people person" someone says they are, working with people is a difficult thing to do. It takes study, practice, patience and an openness to vulnerability. Michael Jordan once said, "I've missed more than 9,000 shots in my career. I've lost almost 300 games. 26 times, I've been trusted to take the game winning shot and missed. I've failed over and over and over again in my life. And that is why I succeed." The same is true with relationships. With every mistake and every effort you learn a bit more. Leadership, like any sport, takes deliberate practice.

 **INSTANT REPLAY**

To summarize, the two sides of the mirror in selling are the science and the art. The differentiator is one's stance toward the customer. On the science side, you are focused on getting an order. On the art side, you are focused on meeting the customer's needs. It is easy to see that once on the art side of the mirror there is a real danger that the activity that enabled the salesperson to get there in the first place will become just another temporary step in their dealing-closing methodology. At that point they are right back to the science side.

In leadership, the same principles hold true where the customer is replaced by the organization. So often leaders are obsessed with their own way of doing things or their own solution-set for delivering the company's strategic agenda. When leaders are captivated by their own image in the mirror, they fail to listen to employees who may provide valuable insight into a different or improved way of doing things. They also fail to develop the capabilities of the organization to empower them not only to meet the strategic objectives but to surpass them in ways they have yet to imagine.

Just as in sales, in leadership, relationships come first. And not the flighty "pleased to meet you so I can check off the box that I communicated" relationship, but lasting, thoughtful relationships in which the leader is the experienced advisor who teaches and is taught, who shares as well as listens and who challenges the status quo.

In the art of selling we are invested in our customers when we consistently work toward their best interest. We determine a common definition of success and a means to track it, we measure performance and communication, we get clear on roles, responsibilities and accountabilities, and we have a functional escalation path. We don't always need a scorecard to track these indices, but they should be part of our internal criteria for success.

In the art of leadership the exact same principles apply, but instead of working toward the interest of the customer, leaders work toward the interest of the organization, including a shared vision, strong two-way communications, clarity around roles, responsibilities and accountabilities and a way to escalate issues when things get sideways.

One of the hardest things to do as a leader is to say "I don't know." Many leaders stumble at this juncture because they are certain that they must be the creator of all solutions or they will lose credibility. Mastering the science and the art of leadership takes time. Through that experience one learns that while the art can certainly result in repeat sales, it is earned customer loyalty that is the real differentiator. When considering the art of leadership, we can also say that 10,000 hours of quality experience is needed. It requires learning the ropes as a manager before taking the helm as leader. At that point the journey has just begun.

The ability to teach your staff, to provide new insights, to guide and mentor, only comes once you have your bachelor's in the science of leadership and your master's in the art of leadership. It is at that point that you enter the space where you have the presence of mind, agility, wit, composure and acumen to even-handedly teach others. In the art of leadership you must have the ability to teach, the vulnerability to say "I am wrong," and the openness to be taught. In Section III we'll explore in depth exactly what it means to be a leader and ways in which you can situate yourself securely on the art side of the mirror—if you are up for the challenge.

THE LEADERSHIP CHALLENGE

*"Leaders must be close enough to relate to others,
but far enough ahead to motivate them."*

—JOHN C. MAXWELL

CHAPTER FIVE

BREAK ON THROUGH TO THE OTHER SIDE

One could argue that leadership is a quality more than a role, and individual contributors and managers alike can demonstrate strong leadership skills regardless of their role. While I agree with this belief, there is a strong positive correlation between the responsibilities of running a region, business unit or entire company and opportunities to grow as a leader and demonstrate leadership qualities. I believe that it is precisely by climbing the ladder of successive responsibilities—whether commercial, operational, or people oriented—that one becomes an expert in a field, making enough mistakes and learning enough lessons to finally take on the mantle of leadership. While there are certainly classes and books that teach leadership, you can only become one through the school of real world experience.

I will list some of the primary characteristics of leadership and expand on a few by relating some personal stories. I'll say upfront that for me, the art of leadership boils down to three primary qualities that cut across all leader capabilities. Without the willingness to powerfully develop these qualities, prospective leaders need not apply. The qualities are: the courage to self-reflect, the willingness to transform yourself, and the ability to connect with others—in that order. Self-reflection must come before self-transformation. Self-reflection and self-transformation then enable honest and genuine connection with others.

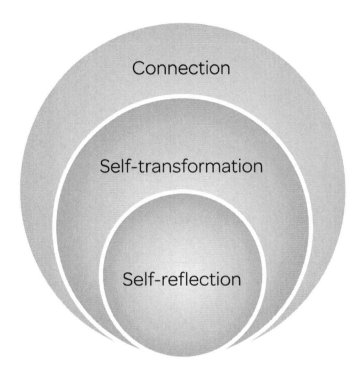

Self-reflection for most people is a frightening thing. This explains the popularity of tools like the Myers-Briggs Type Indicator (MBTI), DiSC, Predictive Index (PI), FIRO-B and other preference and personality indicators. I am a believer in the proper use of these tools as they can help uncover internal drivers that are essential in not only describing but predicting work behavior, attitudes and potential of individuals and groups at all organizational levels. However, these tools appeal to users through a pop approach that takes the sting out of self-analysis with sanitized profiles of the user. Most people take these assessments once, read them through and file them away, perhaps showing them to their friends or spouse as an affirmation to how accurate the description is. In short, they are often used as parlor tricks. They certainly aren't meant to be used that way, but a fear of true introspection prevents many people from using them to their full potential. Many adults don't find the time for true introspection until they are sitting on a therapist's couch.

More frightening than self-reflection is self-transformation. As I have noted several times, real transformation—especially at the personal level—can be painful, and most people simply would rather have a root canal. On an individual level, this fact is sad enough. For a leader it can be devastating since their actions, behaviors and decisions originate from their personal preferences and impact sizeable parts of a business and even external parties, including customers and competition.

My dad used to tell me, "Kid, don't forget where you came from." Literally he meant the North side of Chicago; figuratively, he meant that I should never stray from my values and should always remember my Midwest upbringing and the unique culture of that area. "Don't forget where you came from," was a reminder to me that no matter where I go in life or how high up a corporate ladder I may choose to climb, I should never think too highly of myself, and I should always remember how the average guy thinks, feels and lives. I do believe that one leadership skill that has differentiated me from other leaders is an ability to take a vision and strategy from the upper echelons of a company and make it relevant all the way down to the shop floor, find the gaps and make it happen, end-to-end. I don't say this as a self-congratulatory remark, but because I think this one leadership skill is paramount to all others—at least it was for me. It is the skill that propelled me to cross from the science side of the mirror to the art side. We can simply call it the ability to connect. The key to connection is that it is a two-way mechanism. Leaders must be able to share and listen in equal measure.

PROFILING A LEADER

A leader is as a person who motivates and inspires his or her staff. Their deep care for the organization and the people in it should be evident in their actions and words. A strong leader is also charismatic, tough-willed and smart. A strong leader has excellent communication skills and an ability not only to spot and attract talent, but to develop it. And finally, a strong leader has a vision for the future. This may seem like a cheesy job description; it's all Mother Goose and apple pie stuff. When we peel back the generalities and feel-good jargon, what do we have left? What really is a leader?

For one thing, we should acknowledge that leaders are vested with a certain amount of authority, either formally through a hierarchical system or informally through influence. But here lies the clincher. Power is attributed. Power is vested in people by others. Power is not organic. A leader's true power is granted to him or her through trust. In an organization, people have to *trust* their leaders to lead. I am sure we have all seen the sad result of someone who had the title of leader but whose staff refused to grant them the rights and privileges of that role because they did not trust them. Although a leader may be given the responsibility to make decisions on the organization's behalf, the staff decides (passively or aggressively) if they will follow and support those decisions.

> *"Everybody's got to bring something to the people they lead because nobody can make you a leader but the people who follow you."*
>
> —WOODY SESSOMS, SVP, Global Enterprise, Cisco Systems

Tightly nestled in that attributed power are unspoken rules and sometimes well-documented policies about accountabilities—expectations the leader has to live up to as well as expectations about how the staff should respond. Accountabilities are a type of contract between the leader and their stakeholders (organization, shareholders and customers). They are the rules of the game. When a leader fails to play by the rules of the game they lose the trust of their stakeholders. When that trust is gone, morale and productivity drop, shareholders sell off their investments or put pressure on the board for change, and customers find other companies or brands they can entrust their loyalties to.

For the most part, what we think about leadership has been preprogrammed into us by the major institutions in our lives and then built upon through our own experiences in the workplace. For me, being part of sport teams provided a paramilitary-like set of experiences and results. For others it may be school, military, church or family. It is also principally influenced by leaders, good and bad, that we have worked for or seen in action. Nearly everyone can name one or two managers who have had a major influence on their work lives and why they considered them to be a good leader. It is a natural tendency for new leaders to model prior leaders who have influenced them—again, for better or worse.

With these dynamics in mind, let's consider the seven characteristics of a strong leader:

- **Role Model:** Leaders are expected to be role models for the rest of the company. An overly aggressive leader will spawn a command-and-control culture, a skeptical leader will generate an analytical culture and an open leader will produce a collaborative culture. All this is not to say that leaders single-handedly create a company's culture, but they have a huge impact and that impact grows depending on the organization's willingness to follow the leader's example.

> *"And leading from the front I guess is leading by example, and I think people follow leaders that are willing to get their hands dirty, roll their sleeves up, put the work in, and to actively support the efforts of the team, good and bad."*
>
> —JERE BROWN, CEO, Americas, Dimension Data

- **Balanced Strategist/Tactician:** A strong leader understands the importance of tactics backed by a robust strategy and can rally a team to develop a strategy that is feasible for both the near and long term. A strong leader also understands the criticality of being able to execute a strategy. While a leader may not necessarily build the strategy or execute the plan, they will oversee the development and implementation.

> *"So the question is, 'How can you bring out the best in others?' Part of the way you do that is by bringing out the best in yourself. When you're your best, that inspires people."*
>
> —LARRY LIBERTY, Ph.D., The Liberty Consulting Team

- **Strategic Talent Scout:** Strong leaders gather the best people around them to ensure success for the enterprise. They scout for talent and continually develop the talent in those around them through coaching. A leader seeks out people who have strengths where he or she has weaknesses;

people who have firm opinions but are also team players. A strong leader hires up as opposed to down. True to the mantra, "you are only as strong as your weakest link," "A" players hire A players or better, while B players hire C players and C hire D players. People also tend to hire people like themselves, so as a leader gathers a leadership team around him or her, their biases will be replicated in those they hire. A strong leader is aware of this tendency and consciously hires and develops diverse leaders who balance their style.

It's a good idea to perform a "talent audit" to see how many "A, B, C and D" players you have on your team.

- **Consummate Coach:** As a coach, a strong leader is willing to have a way to share their knowledge. This may come across as teaching for some leaders, preaching for others and mentoring yet for others. Leaders as coaches tend to be opinionated about what is right and what will work, and they aren't afraid to say it. They are also are not afraid to correct their course if they should be proven wrong. As a coach, a strong leader teaches and, more importantly, is teachable.

- **Differential Motivator:** Strong leaders tend to have organizations that will follow them to hell and back if needed. They inspire fierce loyalty and respect which, in turn, inspires staff to relentlessly drive toward delivery. This motivation stems from one or more extraordinary qualities the leader publicly demonstrates in a powerful way. It may be their genuine care for staff, a genius for innovation, or an indefatigable desire to win.

A key force in the ability to motivate and inspire is the ability to communicate with impact. This is the difference between degrees of leadership. In engineering and science industries, for instance, many leaders are weak communicators and are still able to succeed. But for those with strong communication skills, the differential is wide.

- **Credible Expert:** A strong leader must have enough expertise in their field and a track record of success to garner credibility from their stakeholders. There are plenty of examples of leaders without credibility, but they are all short stories and they all end badly. It is through expertise that a leader can synthesize the contextual and mission critical aspects of their business into a cogent vision and strategy. If a leader does not have the expertise themselves, they know where to find it. A leader's credibility is put to the test in times of crisis. A leader without expertise and experience (which are the building blocks of credibility) will falter during a crisis.

- **Courageous Steward:** Finally, strong leaders have guts. They have the courage to make bold decisions, take risks and shoulder the burden if everything should fall apart. The public likes to lambast CEOs for their high salaries and bonuses, but good leaders are brave men and women who take on a Faustian pact with the company that can be paraphrased as follows: "In exchange for devoting all of his or her time, expertise and brain power to the enterprise, the company will take the worry of money off the table." Leaders metaphorically forfeit their lives for the company. The higher a leader climbs, the more that leader is expected to give. The irony is the more responsibility a leader has, the less flexibility he or she has.

The following graphic illustrates the seven characteristics and three qualities of a leader. At the core of all the key leadership characteristics are reflection, transformation, and connection.

SITTING ON THE DOCK OF THE BAY

Technically speaking, there are differences between leaders and managers, but often times it is in title only. A good manager will have at least some leadership skills. Manager roles are typically proving grounds for leaders. Becoming a first line sales manager was another of life's defining moments for me, one long crucible moment.

One of my former VP's started his career in the Navy. He told me of a time when he had to board a hostile vessel and ended up looking down the barrel of a gun. He said that was a terrifying and defining moment for him. He said the day he became a sales manager was an equally terrifying and defining moment.

I thought it was telling that despite his Naval Academy training there was something about the visceral reality and deep complexity of leading people that took him off guard, much like looking down the barrel of a gun. For me this illustrates the fact that there are some realities that can't be simulated. True leadership skills are role-modeled and developed through experience. Some people are predisposed by past experiences and an open mindedness to manage the learning curve faster than others. These people have a type of leadership DNA. With or without that DNA, enough focus and determination coupled with the correct support systems, role modeling and experience can make many people into strong leaders. It may not be easy, but it is possible.

Becoming a first line manager is like becoming a parent. Like a mother or father to their children, a first line manager becomes a role model for their staff. And just like new parents find that some of the things they say to their kids remind them of how their parents spoke to them, a new manager will often fall back on the impact their first managers had on them. New leaders consciously or unconsciously take on traits from the first managers in their careers.

My own management experience began when I was 29. I was working for Deltak, a training firm that provided multi-media Information Technology training solutions. My first management role with Deltak was as a new branch manager in San Francisco. Keep in mind I was moving to Northern California from the Midwest where the winters drop to -20 degrees F. We moved into a beautiful upper floor condo in the Marina. We had a view of the Golden Gate Bridge and Alcatraz from a deck on the roof of the house. I built the deck myself. It became my reflection stoop.

The whole experience was pretty scary. Not that I built a deck on the roof of an apartment in the middle of earthquake country, but that we had spent a tremendous amount of money on that 1200 square foot apartment. Today the same place would probably go for close to ten times what we paid. At that point in my career, though, I was leveraged to the gills. So after a long stressful day, I'd sit on the deck with my wife and sip a glass of wine. We'd watch the sun set over the Golden Gate Bridge and the stresses of the day and the worries of covering our mortgage would just melt away. I learned the value of getting away from the stresses of work and to enjoy the moment.

On my first day, I walked into the San Francisco branch of Deltak and made my own introductions. My intent was to begin to establish trust and connection with the new team. My boss had not flown out, so it was just me introducing myself. While this may sound insensitive on my boss's part, it was actually good in my eyes. His not being there allowed me to show that I was there to make an investment in my team and that I didn't need my boss to lend me his credibility and introduce me as "their new head honcho." I showed up as me. I made my introductions in my own way and began to convey the message that my tenure with them was going to be about me working with them and not me working through someone else. For me, this is a key leadership lesson. The underlying principle is that behavior trumps words. People will remember, judge and model actions more than speeches. Somewhere along the line they will ask themselves, do I want to follow this person? Do I want to vest authority in them, do I want to hold up to my accountabilities on their behalf, do I want to trust them?

At that time Deltak focused on the information technology training business. Some of the staff had been around awhile. There were probably 20 people who reported to me, including salespeople and consultants. I was 29 years old and the next closest in age to me was 35. The oldest employee was 52. I can tell you, it was pretty unnerving. I felt like everyone was scrutinizing me—who does this kid think he is? As a new manager I was sure of my sales abilities and I was confident in my knowledge and skill set, but I had to learn how to apply my knowledge and skills to an incredibly diverse group of team members who all had different needs. I also had to adjust to the West Coast after coming from the Midwest. Let me tell you, it's not just the weather that's different. While I enjoyed the free thinking and culture, I missed the family oriented feel of the Midwest and the tight-knit communities. There were plenty of sushi restaurants and wine bars, but you'd be hard pressed to find a proper tavern.

Recognizing I had a steep learning curve to manage and wanting to be my best, I went to my boss, the president of the company, and requested management training.

"Bob," I pleaded, "I need some training."

"George," he replied, "I can send you to classes for a week or two and you can read all the books that have been written on managing, but it's just something that you've got to go do."

I felt like a drowning man with someone at the side of the pool shouting, "kick your legs and paddle!"

"How about throwing me a fricken' life jacket," I felt like saying. Not being one for career-limiting moves, I nodded and decided to buckle down for the ride. I wished there was a smart pill or textbook I could put under my pillow to transform me into first a competent manager and then a strong leader. I was learning that life and business were variable and the best way to learn to ride the ups and downs, wild turns, sudden stops and yes, smooth cruises, was to live it and learn from it. Similar to how I learned the science and art of sales, I was determined to learn the science and art of leadership. I watched my colleagues, took coaching from anyone sage enough to offer it, kept my eyes wide open and learned from a ton of mistakes.

THE MARINES HAVE LANDED

In those early management days at Deltak I worked with a gentleman named Lynn Terry, who was also from Chicago. Lynn was 52 at the time and I was barely 30. He was ex-military, a Marine. I would say ex-Marine but as Lynn said, "To die a marine is to live forever."

I'm not sure Lynn knew what to think about this young manager from Chicago. He told me that the only reason he tolerated me at first was because whenever we went on sales calls together, we would always close the deal. Lynn and I closed deals with Chevron, Bank of America, Wells Fargo other major accounts up and down Market Street in downtown San Francisco. If there's one thing a Marine respects, its results. Lynn and I got results.

During my time with Deltak, Lynn and I became great friends. He was very much a mentor to me. He would tell me his stories and cap them off with these great Marine expressions. When we had a tough sales call he'd say, "Courage is enduring for one moment longer"; when we had landed a difficult account he'd say, "The marines have landed. The situation is well in hand." The two big lessons Lynn taught me were, "It's all about the troops," and, "leadership emerges in crucible moments."

The first notion was intuitive for me. It was something I knew before my first day, which is why I wanted to introduce myself instead of having my boss introduce me. I wanted to connect with my team right off the bat and then nurture a relationship of mutual trust. Perhaps it was something I learned from my football years at NIU—coaches lose ballgames, players win ball games. Perhaps I learned it from my parents, perhaps from that Italian restaurant. Wherever I learned it from, I knew there was no chance I was going to lead anyone without first establishing a relationship with them and earning their trust.

Lynn would say, "If you take care of your troops, they'll take care of you." Lynn described failure in this area as resulting in friendly fire. That is, if the troops feel like you did not stand up for them, they are likely to shoot you in the back. That's as true in the armed forces as it is in business. There are many ways to take care of your troops, such as shutting down unnecessary work (like data requests), giving praise and credit where praise and credit are due, never taking credit for someone else's work, defending your team, taking the proverbial "bullet" for the team and celebrating success.

One thing we always did (in fact it was a mantra for the team) was to "Work hard, play hard, and have a good time." When there were deadlines to hit, numbers to make, we focused hard and got the job done. When the goal was made, we celebrated, and we celebrated well. Importantly, I also made it a point to involve significant others in social events like Christmas parties, team celebrations and strategy offsite meetings. During the "regular season," if my team had a business dinner, I always made sure they each ordered a dessert specifically to take home to their spouse, partner or children. At times I would write handwritten notes to the significant others acknowledging their often unheralded contribution. You wouldn't believe how much a simple "thank you" means to people.

The second notion of crucible moments was something I was actually living in an extended way but couldn't truly appreciate for what it was at the moment. I was too close to the matter to really understand it. It commanded all my focus and I could only sense the wider context. What I couldn't see was that the constant pressure of managing our West Coast operations and people was actually giving me a treasure trove of experiences that I would be able to draw upon later. It was making me a better leader. It wasn't until many years later that I truly appreciated this.

Robert J. Thomas the author of *Crucibles of Leadership: How to Learn from Experience and Become a Great Leader* relates that the most explosive learning moments in life are when you're under the most pressure. He uses the example of fighter pilots. They discovered that the best fighter pilots were not necessarily those who do well in the simulators. As well as a simulator approximates reality, it can't replicate the intense pressure of a real flight situation like jetting through the air at ungodly speeds with someone shooting at you. Those are skills that can't be assessed in a simulator. The only way to assess how a pilot will do in that type of situation is for them to experience that type of situation—in reality and not simulation. It is during those intense times, crucible moments, that a pilot's real stuff is revealed. As it turns out Lynn was a good 25 years ahead of his time—sound wisdom is ageless.

And so Bob, my boss, was right. I just had to do it. I made mistakes in those years and learned more lessons than I would have in a lifetime of reading books or attending training. It really was something I just had to go do. From branch manager I went on to district manager and then to regional manager. Although I stayed right there in San Francisco, my leadership skills jumped forward light years. I'm not saying things were easy or everything I did was golden, but sitting on the deck each night, the mentoring from Lynn, and attending to the troops all helped me put things into perspective. Life and work can sometimes feel like one long crucible moment and we have to take it like that—a defining moment to test our mettle and an opportunity to grow as leaders.

 **INSTANT REPLAY**

While some people may claim the qualities of leadership are innate, I maintain the art of leadership is arrived at and refined through experiences accumulated through a journey, which in business typically progresses from individual contributor to manager to leader. Unfortunately, there is no smart pill for leadership; it takes 10,000 or 20,000 hours of experience just to become good. While there are many capabilities of a leader, the three qualities which cut through all of them are: self-reflection, self-transformation and connection—in that order.

Leaders are life-vested with authority that is attributed by their stakeholders. They work within guidelines of accountabilities and the primary currency with their stakeholders is trust. They also have a tremendous impact on the businesses they operate within, on a wide range of stakeholders from employees to customers, and, most importantly, on up and coming leaders who will model their behaviors. Seven key characteristics of a strong a leader are:

- Role Model

- Balanced Strategist/Tactician

- Strategic Talent Scout

- Consummate Coach

- Differential Motivator

- Credible Expert

- Courageous Steward

Being a manager for the first time can be an eye-opening experience. There is nothing that can really prepare you for the reality. The key to navigating your way through the myriad of experiences that will come your way is to be open to learning. Look for mentors/role models; look for examples in your peers and even your staff. Crossing from the science of leadership side of the mirror to the art of leadership side is not a smooth transition. Often times it will involve breaking glass (perhaps the mirror itself) and making mistakes. As a mentor and friend of mine, Lynn Terry, would say: "It doesn't matter that you fell down. What matters is how fast you get back up."

Two key lessons I learned about the art of leadership in my early years as a manager at Deltak were to take care of the troops and the importance of crucible moments. Taking care of the troops meant creating a strong connection with them based on trust and authenticity. If I took care of them, they would take care of me. We worked hard and played hard. I also learned that the person who showed up to work every day often did so because they had someone at home to help them maintain a balance and to be a helpmate to manage the ups and downs of life. Extending that person at home a genuine "thank you" through gestures both big and small helped me to fuse my connection with my team.

Crucible moments are intense moments we all experience in which we learn tremendous lessons about work and/or life and about ourselves. Crucible moments can't be taught through classes, books or even simulators—though practice and structure may smooth out some of the rough edges. The only thing that teaches crucible moments are crucible moments themselves. Similarly, leadership is about doing. You can't become a strong leader by watching from the sidelines, reading a book or letting others make mistakes on your behalf. Leadership is a do-it-yourself proposition.

CHAPTER SIX

WHAT YOU MAY HAVE MISSED IN GRAD SCHOOL

Leadership roles are not entry-level positions. Leadership roles come through a natural career progression, typically starting with individual contributor, or maybe a team lead, then progressing to manager then on to a leader. Along the way there are multiple moves up and down and diagonally within and across organizations, all adding to the depth and breadth of a person's skill sets and experience, ultimately preparing them for a leadership role.

Regardless of how someone progresses to a leadership position, I would advise taking a leadership role with eyes wide open. Too many people assume the transition from manager to leader is a simple job transition, but the reality is leadership is much more than a job; it is an entire way of thinking and being. The transition from manager to leader requires substantial sacrifice and effort.

In this chapter I'll speak very transparently about some of those nuances and describe six key leadership realities I learned the hard way.

THE BLINK TEST

Leaders are faced with difficult situations on a daily basis. Whether it's an internal issue such as an underperforming employee, an underperforming segment, a disappointed client, or an external issue such as a media crisis, a public safety issue or disappointed consumers, a strong leader has to be able to handle difficult situations without flinching.

Early in my career I learned that the public, customers and staff would make challenging requests or present difficult situations and then watch to see how the leader handles it. This is the "blink test" of leadership and it can happen anytime, come from anywhere and involve anyone. The proper response isn't about having the right answer; it is all about how you react. How you react will speak volumes about you and will tell the person on the other side of the table how seriously to take you, what issues they can trust you with and what your hot buttons are. Being defensive, panicking, laying blame on others, shirking from the truth, being evasive or retreating into a shell are all examples of what you don't want to do. What you do want to do is look the person in the eye and give them a straightforward answer based on the truth as you know it.

Sending the right message at the wrong time is the wrong message.

The schoolyard is never far away

A vivid example of the blink test from my own career was when I was negotiating a contract with the United Auto Workers union. At the time they were infamous for using work stoppages, strikes and other strong-arm tactics to get what they wanted. In short, these guys didn't play around.

I remember an appointment I had with one of the heads of the union (we'll call him Jim) to review a proposal I had drawn up on behalf of our company. I went to see Jim in his office. The office was a no frills affair, sparsely and mundanely furnished. What it did have, however, was a large desk and a single chair positioned in front of it.

I was a young salesperson at the time. I imagine I looked like a piece of chum to a hungry, circling shark. I sat down as Jim thumbed through my proposal, looking at the headers, reading a sentence or two. When he got to the end, he held it up by one corner. With his other hand, he reached into his jacket pocket and pulled out a silver Zippo lighter. He said, "This proposal is a piece of sh—." He then lit the proposal on fire.

I started having flashbacks of my Chicago school days facing down bullies. This was the classic scenario of a tough guy throwing out an insult, or even a punch, to see if I would back down or throw one back. I had enough composure to know that although Jim was essentially a bully, he was also the customer and held the cards. As the proposal burned, I realized I had two choices. One was to respond how he wanted me to—storm out of the office, start an argument or react in some other dramatic way. The other was to look him in the eye and act like it was just another day at the office.

As he turned the paper in his fingers so as not to burn himself, I said, "Jim, I get the sense you're not happy with the proposal."

He raised an eyebrow as if to say, "What gave you that impression?"

I continued calmly. "I tell you what, let me work with your team and see what else we can come up with."

"Why don't you just do that?" he replied.

I nodded and left the office. He had learned everything about me he needed to know from that interaction: I wasn't going to scare and I didn't blink. He had achieved his objective for the meeting. Mine, of course, had just begun.

As I walked out of the office, a couple of men from Jim's team came out of an adjacent room and asked me how things went. We huddled in an office and started to confer. I had seen enough detective shows to recognize a "good cop, bad cop" scenario when I saw it. So I worked with the two "good cops" over the next few days to draft a new proposal. However, my real plan was to have them present it to Jim, not me. They did, no Zippo lighters were used, and everything went fine.

In retrospect their tactic was, "Let's play some dramatics to scare this kid and help sweeten the deal for the union." My tactic was, "I'm going to remain calm and negotiate within the parameters my company has established." The result was a deal both parties could accept. The lesson I learned was about the lengths some people will go to test somebody's resolve and how important it is to not blink. Sometimes business interactions are sad extensions of the schoolyard.

The courage of candor

I should point out here that not blinking is different than seeking out conflict or being confrontational. Not blinking is a leadership quality. Not blinking is having the courage to speak the truth when the truth is not always comfortable or convenient. You don't have to be rude to speak the truth, but you do have to have some degree of candor. For instance, new managers sometimes make the mistake of "keeping score" and of not communicating their views. Failing to tell an employee who is underperforming that they are not meeting expectations is doing no one any favors. Avoiding telling a customer that their product or service will be late is not going to make them any happier when the shortfall becomes obvious: in fact, it will make matters worse.

In sharing bad news, tell it quickly—that is, when it happens. Drawing it out, avoiding it or hiding it is poor judgment and weak leadership.

In addition, not blinking does not mean you have to be an emotionless, unfeeling tyrant. Sometimes not blinking is telling a group of people that divesting a part of a business was a difficult decision you struggled with but in the end you had to do what was best for the business. Sometimes not blinking is admitting to emotions and demonstrating you have a heart. Not blinking doesn't mean not feeling, not blinking means owning your responsibilities.

One of the most difficult things I had to do in my career was to downsize a team I had been leading for three years. I had the option of letting the impacted employees know by phone without having to actually meet them face to face. (TelePresence[6] was not invented yet and the early days of video conference calls were very low tech.) I chose instead to fly out to meet each one of them

---

[6] TelePresence is a suite of high definition video and audio technologies which allow persons in different locations to communicate with one another. The resolution of the video and quality of the audio is so high as to make it seem as if both parties are face to face in one room. The first commercially successful TelePresence company emerged in 1993. HP, Cisco and Polycom soon entered the market.

individually to tell them the news in person. It wasn't something I had to do; it was something that as a leader I felt like I should do. There was no company policy compelling me to have personal conversations. What compelled me was the conviction that my staff deserved my best, which included me looking them in the eye and letting them know the rationale and the next steps about what was happening.

I remember those long airport terminal walkways as I traveled from city to city, looking at the carpet and escalators, rehearsing in my mind what I was going to say, and playing out possible scenarios. Nothing could prepare me for how the conversations actually occurred. Each conversation was as varied as the people themselves. What was common amongst them all, however, was in the end they each shook my hand and thanked me for seeing them personally. To this day I am struck with a mixed feeling of melancholy and pride when I walk through airport terminals remembering those days—melancholy that I had to let good people go; pride that I was able to do so in person and without blinking.

You can **read** about these types of activities in a manager's training manual because they can be described in a science-like step-by-step process, but you can only **learn** the art of doing them by actually going through the experience yourself. It's not pleasant and therefore managers and leaders alike try to avoid it. If you do avoid it, unfortunately, you only increase the burden upon the people you are letting go. As a leader it's your responsibility to take that hit and to not flinch.

The strength of being vulnerable

Not blinking also means being able to own up to mistakes and being able to talk about failings openly. Being open about shortcomings indicates that you have learned from the past and that you possess a certain amount of self-awareness. It also indicates to the listener that you accept responsibility—sometimes known as the *locus of control*—and that you are human just like them. It gives them permission to be themselves and assures them that they too can learn from their mistakes.

In the final analysis, not blinking is about facing your stakeholders with transparency rooted in experience and self-awareness. You can't fake not blinking; you can only prepare by being open and transparent with your staff and by striving to understand yourself.

THE POWER OF "NO"

A subset to the blink test is the power of saying "no." Often a customer will say "no" to a proposal because they have learned that the salesperson afraid of losing a sale will come back with a better deal. A salesperson without a clear understanding of their economic boundaries and their walk-away position will generally respond with a sweeter deal to every "no" they hear regardless of how economically irresponsible the customer's request may be. Customers understand the power of "no" better than salespeople do.

Know your boundaries and walk-away position in all situations, not just when negotiating a sale.

When I joined Cisco, I quickly saw the need to establish criteria for what a fiscally responsible transaction looked like and to create a Solution Center support team. I immediately began work to put both in place. This was not as simple as setting dollar limits, but rather it involved teaching our sales staff how to numerate and negotiate value exchanges based upon gross margin and not percentage discount. For instance, if a customer agreed to use a single system across all of their sites, we could factor that into the pricing because our support costs would be reduced.

Once we had the value exchange criteria established, it was then a matter of closing the door on exceptions. The only way we would allow an exception was if we extended the terms to all our partners. If, during the analysis, we found that standardizing the exception did not make economic sense and was not applicable to the broader set of channel partners then no exception would be made. There were a lot of exception requests from customers and partners that were denied. I became known as "Dr. No," though I would have preferred to be called "Dr. Know."

The fear amongst the sales team was that our customers and partners would leave in droves once we started to say, "No." What they learned was that when you understood your walk-away position it took all the emotion out of the decision. They also discovered that when they sat down with the customers and were transparent about our boundaries, the customers understood it was about value exchange. It didn't mean they stopped asking for the world, but they weren't so disappointed when we said, "No." By learning to stay firm and consistent, our bottom-line improved and our customers (especially our partners) respected us more. There were, of course, some ruffled feathers and more than once that I had to pass the blink test.

When negotiating, understand that a customer will generally have the most energy and emotion in areas where they have been burned in the past. If you discover those early on, the value exchange process works even better.

One particularly memorable occasion was in negotiating with a mega-retailer who will go unnamed. I had been with Cisco for only a few years when I was called to the headquarters town of this account. They said they wanted to meet with someone who had enough authority to decide the terms of a very large deal. That was me.

My sales operations director, I'll call him Scott, and I arrived at their headquarters. We waited in the lobby for over half an hour. They eventually called us into an over-sized conference room and we waited another half hour. The CIO entered with our local account manager and sat at one end of a long boardroom table. Scott and I were on the other side. Although we were not directly facing each other, the CIO could still look me straight in the eye. He started: "George, I'm glad you're here to make the decision. I'd like you to review the overall transaction and tell me what you're going to do to meet my price targets."

I looked the CIO in the eye and replied, "This could be a very short discussion given what you've asked for." I then explained that the proposal was not an economically-responsible deal that I could take back to the corporation and call it a win/win situation.

"Well, wait a second," he said. "I'm telling you this is exactly what I need in order for me to make this work, and you're telling me you can't do it. I thought you could make the decision. That's why I asked you here."

I had to reiterate that while I was the person who could make the decision, based on the data we were both looking at the decision was no. From there we launched into an exercise of examining the numbers and discussing potential value exchanges. In the end, however, what they were asking for was far beyond the boundaries and the walk-away position we had established for the deal. I could not say "Yes," to an exception, especially of this magnitude, without violating my personal standard and acting in contradiction to everything I had been enforcing with my team. Ethically and financially it would be wrong. I stood firm.

At one point during the discussion he stopped, literally mid-sentence. He furrowed his brow and glared at the account manager, Joe. Joe by that time had gone way dark on the other side of the moon. Even though he was paid by Cisco, he might as well have been employed by the customer. This often happens with regionally-based salespeople who are assigned to mega-accounts. They get drawn deep into the environment, which can be both good and bad. When you put people onsite, they rapidly adopt the customer's culture and start to drink the Kool-Aid. So he turned to Joe and said, as if I wasn't in the room, "I don't think he's listening to me." Then he turned back to me and said, "George, tell me again why you're not going to meet my price demand."

In a very low, calm voice, I replied, "This is not an economically responsible deal, nor do we have any value-based exchange that I can take back to the corporation that even John Chambers would approve." I mentioned John because I knew he would want to escalate to the biggest name he could. I therefore invited him to call John Chambers if he felt he needed to.

We continued for some time. Then my sales director, Scott, thought he came up with a unique angle. He said, "Sir, you need to look at it this way."

The CIO glanced at him and barked, "You're interrupting me." Now Scott really thought he had a way of calming the storm so he kept going. The mercury pretty much hit 212 degrees at that point. The CIO blew his stack, got up and stormed out of the room.

In the next few moments we sat there in the awkward silence, pulling together our notes and paper, waiting for the next shoe to drop. Suddenly the door opened. From the door the CIO told the account manager, Joe, to join him in the hall. Through the closed door we could clearly hear him say, "I want you to remove him from the building now. He's never, ever to step another foot into this building."

He opened the door, looked at me and said, "George, I want to thank you for your time. We're going to agree to disagree. And you can tell Mr. Chambers he's going to get a call."

I said fine. We shook hands. By this time it was 3:30 pm and our plane was due to leave at four o'clock. There was no way we could make the flight, so we caught the Saturday morning flight. The CIO ended up calling John who proposed we bring in our Senior VP of Technical Support as a mediator to negotiate the overall deal.

The point to all this is not about whether or not the deal was landed. The point is as a leader it was my responsibility to uphold the standards I held my own staff to. I was completely transparent with our customer, and I did not let the size of the account and how much product they purchase sway my decision. The easiest thing for me to have done anywhere along the way was to have just said "Yes," and given in to their demands.

One leadership lesson here is about holding firm to your values. Another, however, is about the cost of holding to those values. What I have found is that you can burn through a lot of emotional capital in the process of getting a deal landed after the customer has said "No" 10 times. The marketing definition of emotional capital is the emotional value people invest in brands. In negotiating with a customer you add to and take away from the emotional investment the customer has made with your company as a brand.

If you know you are eventually going to get to "yes" and give in to some or all of the customer's demands, do it quickly. If you take months to negotiate what you may think is a win-win deal, you may in fact get the business but it will take years to rebuild the lost emotional capital.

In the example above, while I can say I was pleased I did not commit Cisco into an unwise deal, I can also say I was displeased that we burned so much emotional capital with our customer. It was a difficult situation and I had to make a difficult decision. As a leader, those situations and decisions come on a daily basis.

PIPELINE FREEZE

In Chicago where the winters could reach a wind chill of -20° on a routine basis, there was always the danger that water would freeze in the pipes. When water freezes, it expands. Water expanding in pipes means pipelines will bust; never a good thing. In human behavior I refer to pipeline freeze as the phenomenon of freezing in the presence of executive leadership or when in difficult situations. The person doesn't burst, of course, but the situation becomes awkward and the optimal outcome is rarely met. In fact, pipeline freeze is almost the exact opposite reaction of what needs to be happening at that point in time. For instance, an up-and-coming employee freezing in the presence of the CEO isn't likely to come across as the sharp, motivated employee their peers know them as. A nervous, stammering salesperson doesn't exactly instill confidence in a customer either. Pipeline freeze happens to everybody, especially salespeople and people new to an organization.

I recall a time when I was working with a young, upwardly mobile salesperson at Cisco, we'll call him Brian. Brian was motivated, smart and driven and had more than one good idea about how to improve things. On the development side, he wasn't the most organized person, but he was diligent, followed-up methodically, and was well respected by his customers.

We had an important executive meeting via TelePresence to discuss some complex matters with which Brian was involved. If you have not used a TelePresence room, just know that TelePresence is basically the I-Max of the video conferencing world. The rooms are set up like intimate auditoriums, usually seating four to sixteen people. The screens are high-definition, as is the audio. The audio is set up directionally, so when someone on the right side of the screen speaks, the audio pipes through on the right side of the room. It's very intimate and feels like you are there in person.

So we're setting up the room on our side of the call. Ten minutes before the CEO and CIO are due to dial in, Brian provides our team in San Jose with the context and objectives for the call. He does a good job, a little quick, but a good job nonetheless. You could tell he was eager to be done with it. When he finished, he said, "Okay, if you need anything I'll be just outside the door."

I said, "No, you're in the room."

He stared at me a second and blinked once or twice. He was having pipeline freeze. He was comfortable enough talking with the Cisco team in the TelePresence room, but then being in the room with the CEO clearly made him nervous.

"You're in the room," I repeated. "We need you here to help field questions and be part of the action items. Just take a seat and relax."

He sat down and began to loosen up in the few minutes left before the call.

Brian later told me the hallway chatter before the TelePresence call was filled with comments like, "Ooh, you get to meet with the CEO," and "Oh, I guess you'll be an Intergalactic Client Director soon." As friendly as the chatter may have been, it didn't help to ease Brian's nerves. The idea of having to interact with the CEO was intimidating for him.

So if one tip is not to blink, another tip is not to let people intimidate you. Although it may be easier said than done, remember all the hard work you went through to earn yourself a seat at the table. One practical tip is to thoroughly prepare. Again, you play like you practice, so practice. Also keep in mind that few executives think of themselves the same way that other people in the organization think of them. That is to say, most executives would be at a loss to understand why anyone would be intimidated by them. They are just people like you and me. The important thing to remember is that as you progress up the ladder, people will become intimidated by you. As a leader, part of your job is to ease that same tension others may feel through communication and connection. There will be more on this subject later.

EXECUTIVE PRESENCE

On the flip side to how we react to leadership presence is the presence we exhibit as leaders. Every prospective leader needs to develop a presence unique to them. Executive presence says, "I am confident, I am supposed to be here, I am relaxed with who I am." People sense executive presence; they may not be able to define it, but they know it when they see it. When someone with executive presence walks into a room, everyone sits up a little straighter. Real executive presence is not based on position or fear; it is based on respect and trust.

 You don't have to be an executive to have executive presence.

The best and simplest way to develop executive presence is by giving yourself permission to role model somebody else. It works like this: Your ability to display presence is based upon snapshots of your behaviors. Everybody has attitudes, beliefs and behaviors. You may not be able to see the first two, but you can certainly see behaviors. Let's say you are in a meeting and you want to ask a question. You could ask a question in two general voices—your own or someone else's. Now, I'm not suggesting you impersonate how someone speaks, I'm saying you should give yourself permission to frame a question as someone you admire might frame it. You could ask a courageous question, an insightful question, a probing question. As you take on the **voice** of someone else, you make a mental transition that begins to allow you to understand the world a bit like they might, to gain some of the confidence you attribute to them and to add to your repertoire of style. These are acts of expansion that will help you develop as a person and a leader and, ultimately, allow you to expand the perception of your presence.

One person I have always respected and emulated is John Chambers. When John speaks to you, you feel like you're the only person in the room. This is true whether you're in a group of four people or in a group of 300 people. John has a way of engaging with people through his eyes, his gestures, his tone and his words that tells people he is interested in who they are and what they have to say. That's a skill I have always admired in John and have sought to model in my own behaviors.

Another technique is to adapt good communication skills, which we will cover more extensively in later chapters. I will say here, however, that the key to communications is building connections. Being authentic, learning to trust yourself and teaching others to trust who you are will help you to build connections and build confidence in yourself over time. You'll also become more comfortable in your own skin in all situations—work and home alike. That confidence and comfort directly extends into executive presence.

THE INTEGRATION AND DISINTEGRATION OF WORK AND LIFE

Twenty years ago if you told me I wasn't going to have a personal life on weekends when I entered into leadership, I would have said, "Bull crap. I'm going to have life balance, play golf on weekends, and spend time with my family and more." Over those twenty years I came to realize that having balance in your life and being a leader are two things that don't naturally blend. This is a special leadership challenge, and it's a tough one to come to terms with. The challenge will pertain to you personally as a leader as well as to your employees.

In today's world the notion of work-life balance has shifted to work-life integration. Work-life balance is the idea that work and life (all things not work) are two separate things and should be held in equal check—or, more to the point, that work life should not exist to the exclusion of personal life. That means you only work when you are in the office or on the clock, and by the same rules you don't conduct personal business while at work. Over the years that mantra has fallen away to the idea that we should find ways to integrate work and life so that one supports the other. The easiest example is how the workspace has invaded the home and vice versa. Today the typical employee has a laptop (now supplemented with tablets and smart phones) they can take home where they have high speed wireless Internet, a personal printer, and a comfortable and quiet place to work. In many ways, homes look a lot like the office. Meanwhile, many company offices now have café's equipped with refrigerators, microwaves and coffee makers; break rooms with comfortable furniture and televisions; and even campuses with fitness centers, running trails and recreational games (ping pong, foosball, board and electronic games). More and more homes look like the office and more and more offices look like the home.

So what does work-life integration mean for a leader? There is no simple answer. With your team, it means understanding their priorities and understanding that having a meaningful and happy life outside of work shouldn't have to come at the expense of a successful career. With you, it means coming to the same understanding. The only way to accomplish this with your staff is to connect with them. The only way to accomplish this with you is to connect with yourself.

And now for the no blinking part: Despite all we want out of work and life, there is one truism with which leaders must come to grips. The higher up you go in a company, the more of you is going to be required for the company. In business, responsibility works inversely with flexibility. The more responsibility you have, the less flexibility you will have. There will come a time in every upwardly mobile person's career when it becomes obvious that the "don't work evenings, weekends and during vacation," rule is meant for others and the expectation for managers and leaders is you put in those extra hours to set the pace for the business.

Many leaders have discovered a whole other work week happens over the weekend. "Online all the time" has forever changed the work-life polarity. Because it is generally solo work, weekend work can be very productive. Businesses like FedEx® have created a high margin, cottage industry catering to the needs of leaders who now wait till the last minute and in many cases toil away over the weekends. My dad taught me that for a customer there is a big difference between 5:00 pm Friday and 9:00 am Monday morning; for the person who is delivering the work or product, that difference is another 40 plus hours to perfect the end product or result. High-performers everywhere are more than aware of this hidden weekend. They leverage it for everything they can, but at what cost?

Command-and-control managers tend to be poor in the work-life integration camp, because whenever anyone on their team is failing, they step in and do their job for them. Because failure is not an option, they take on a tremendous workload which yields short term results but leads to work-life *dis*integration.

Now, this does not mean that you can't have a life and a career. It means that if your life outside of work is important to you (hint, it should be) and if career progression is important to you, then you will need to carefully manage and organize your time and resources to do both. Do not expect these priorities to align themselves all on their own. Managing work-life integration will require effort on your part. In the eighties and nineties "time management" was all the rage. Personally, I am disappointed to see this drop out of corporate development curriculum. Everyone could use some old-fashioned time management lessons.

I can't promise you'll never work over a weekend or during the evening or find yourself stealing time during a vacation, but if done correctly, a few uninterrupted hours on a Saturday or Sunday can be as productive as an entire weekend locked away in your home office. In addition, because of the portability of secure online access—wireless laptops, tablets, smart phones—low intensity work can be done pretty much anywhere, anytime. More than once I have caught up with e-mails sitting with the family in the den watching a show. Finally, when managing work-life integration, keep the right expectations on your team. Make sure they are accountable for their own work and let them make mistakes. *Always remember your staff will be watching your example.*

LETTING GO

Before we begin this section, I'd like to ask a question. The question is: How would you rate yourself (1 being low and 5 being high) in the area of actively performance managing your staff? Why? What could you do to improve? I frequently ask myself this question, not as a form of self-interrogation but rather as a reminder to focus on Job One. Below are some lessons I learned in this area.

There are two kinds of letting go when it comes to people development: one is helping your best people advance further in the business—hence letting go of your best people so they can develop; the other is moving underperformers out of the business—hence the more traditional usage of "letting someone go." Unselfishly ensuring your best performers progress through the ranks is a sign of strength in leadership. Unflinchingly exiting people with dignity and respect is another sign of strength.

From my experience, most managers early in their career keep a personal score card in their head about everyone on their team. The issue is they keep it secret and fail to tell their individual team members until it's too late. The fact is they have already formed an opinion. To HR's lament, that opinion is rarely documented. The reality is everyone, high performers and poor performers want to know where they stand. It is our responsibility as leaders to set the context and meaning to the term "performance."

Development

Helping a team member grow into their full potential requires more effort than many would think. The natural tendency for a manager is to hold on to their best performers. In some companies a paradox exists in which the best performers never progress because they do their work so well their bosses will not let them move on to bigger and better things. This type of selfishness can be as damaging to a company as tolerating underperformers. A high performing employee who is held back will eventually become embittered and leave the company. The company not only loses the employee's current skills and talents but all their potential. The company also loses the employee's vast business and social network. In addition, other employees will take note. The implicit message becomes, "If you perform well, you will never be promoted." That's poor incentive to grow a business.

Investing in an employee to help them grow and develop for the next level has multiple positive impacts. First, you strengthen the company. A sign of a strong leader is that they can develop a feeder pool for talent. For the leader this may seem exhausting . . . because it is. Finding and developing talent only to have them move on to other roles in a company is hard work, but it is the work leaders need to be involved in. There is nothing more satisfying than to look across a company and see people you helped to grow and develop helping the company to grow and develop.

By developing staff and allowing them to move onward, you send a message to your team that if they perform well they will be rewarded. When people believe there is a real future for them in a company, the quality of their work and the level of their dedication will increase exponentially.

Consider taking this challenge. If you hire and develop great talent, you should take one or two of your best people and move them to better opportunities and then go back out there and do it again. While this will be frustrating in the short run, over time that experience will turn into an art. You will become known as a leader who takes care of his or her people and improves the overall capabilities of the organization.

Dismissals

As a leader you will have people in the organization who need to move on to other jobs for which they have more aptitude. That's the polite way of saying you will have under-performing staff you will need to let go. A peek into any management book will tell you performance management is relatively straightforward. There's a process of do's and don'ts, documentation, letters of concern and performance improvement plans. What books can't quite convey is that in a performance management discussion you are talking to another human being who you probably like and with whom you have a working relationship. There is nothing in the textbook that can prepare you for the emotion and outcomes in these kinds of conversations where you are telling someone they need to improve or that their skills and strengths don't meet the job requirements and it is time they leave the business.

When I was coming up through the ranks of management we practiced a technique very much in vogue back then, but which has become less popular in the last 20 years. It's called "coaching somebody out of the business." It requires a certain degree of finesse, which may be why it has gone by the wayside. It also requires hard work and, in our terms, more art than science. Let me offer an example.

"Stan, you've had a pretty good run here, but you've missed the last couple of quarters and your performance (with specific examples) is continuing to decline. We're at a fork in the road. I really want to see you be successful, but I'm not sure this is the right job for you given your skills and abilities.

One alternative is we could put you on a performance improvement plan which will have some specific gates tied to areas of improvement and results. If you miss any of those gates, it will immediately trigger an exit plan. The other alternative is for us to have a discussion about how you can drive your career to the next level elsewhere. Should you choose this option, I will put together a nice exit package so you can get your next career started."

In coaching someone out of the business the special skill is to be unflinchingly honest and enable the employee to make the decision. I remember the first time I needed to coach someone out of the business. As a brand new manager this was one of the hardest discussions in my life, but it had to be done. It was a crucible moment for me and for the other person involved. The individual was by trade and academic background an education consultant who had been promoted into sales. This was a classic example of a manager mistakenly thinking that "anyone can do sales." Despite what her previous manager thought, this individual was not a salesperson and was not showing the aptitude to develop into one. I prepared my documentation and spent an hour and a half explaining to her what sales was about, in what areas she was deficient and why she was not making the numbers. I showed her that while she was a talented and skilled person, her skills did not match the requirements of the job.

Most everyone becomes defensive when shown a perception of reality that differs from their own. This individual was no exception, but after listening, arguing and shedding a few tears she began to accept the case and carefully reconsider her options. She knew that she did not have the necessary skills, and she also knew she was not keen on gaining them. Once presented with the unblinking truth that there were other viable options she could pursue in which she would probably be much happier and more successful, she said, "Okay, I think I'll take option two. I'll look for a career somewhere else."

What I worked hard to make clear during our discussion was that while she did not have the required skills for her current role, she was amply talented in other areas. The misstep wasn't that she was not smart or gifted, the misstep was that her previous manager set up her up to fail by placing her in a role she was not qualified for in the first place; nor did he invest the time to teach and model for her how to become successful.

I firmly believe that with few exceptions people can and will succeed doing what they love to do. The problem is some people end up in roles for which they have no passion and/or for which they have very few qualifications. Sadly, oftentimes they get there because someone puts them there. They then stay there because no one is willing to have the tough discussion with them, explaining that their skills have been mismatched. They are great athletes but playing the wrong position.

An underperforming employee should know how they are performing—especially if their leader has been doing their job and giving them feedback along the way. At one point in my career I was on the receiving end of a performance improvement plan (PIP) and experienced firsthand what it was like to be on the other side of the desk for that discussion. PIP's can actually be positive, which in my case it turned out to be. For me it was a wakeup call that I was not delivering on my obligations. After the discussion I was able to understand what was important to my manager, correct my course and have an outstanding year. That PIP for me was an uncomfortable process, but it had a positive outcome and I was thankful for it.

Weak leaders and managers tend to avoid conflict. They also tend to have uninteresting careers with lackluster results. Avoiding difficult conversations with underperformers will dilute the strength of the company and diminish your leadership brand. I need to be crystal clear here. Being a strong leader is not just about letting people go, it's about the process and how you communicate.

When someone starts to fail, a leader needs to take it very seriously—especially if it is someone the leader has brought in from another part of the company. Leaders need to remember they are always visible. Team members immediately note a leader's lack of accountability. It informs them what behaviors will be tolerated; it indicates how they can expect to be treated and paints a picture of the leader's integrity.

As a footnote to my story, years later I caught up with the individual with whom I had the difficult performance management discussion. She told me that although at the time the conversation was hard for her to digest, she went on to lead a highly successful career in a field for which she had a true passion. She said that conversation put her on a path to success and career fulfillment. For me, there could not have been a better outcome.

My dad used to tell me, "Kid, sometimes you lose and you have to go back and ask why you lost. And when you win, you should also go back and ask why you won." As I progressed through my own career journey I won a lot and I lost a lot. In this chapter I shared the nuances of leadership that sometimes led to me losing and sometimes led to me winning, nuances that not everyone notices, nuances I wished someone had told me about before I ran into them face first.

The blink test is about holding firm to your convictions and values even in the toughest of circumstances. As the expression goes, you don't have to have a great memory if you always tell the truth. In leadership this translates to being as transparent as you can in your dealings with customers, staff, colleagues and shareholders. This will sometimes lead to difficult conversations in which you have to disclose aspects of yourself, provide authentic feedback that may be hard for people to digest and you may even have to say "no" to people who aren't used to hearing that word. Through it all you need to be true to yourself and the standards you have set. The results will be the loyalty of your customers and shareholders, and the respect of your staff and colleagues.

Within the DNA strand scientists and biologists will one day discover the gene which instills fear of authority, or **pipeline freeze**. Part of the leadership curve, or maybe just part of the growing up curve, is becoming comfortable around high-level authority figures. Emerging leaders should understand that existing leaders are just like everyone else. They certainly had to do something different to get where they are, but those attributes should not be a cause for fear or anxiety. In fact, those attributes are likely to be many of the same ones that need to be acquired by anyone on a leadership track. Granted there are a few bullies in the ranks, but that disqualifies them from being true leaders. An important leadership quality is in overcoming your own **pipeline freeze**, but also helping others to overcome theirs.

Executive presence is having a confident demeanor and frame of mind that others can sense. There is no magic pill to developing executive presence. One way is through role modeling; that is, take someone whom you admire and try to model their behavior, including how they seem to think. Another is to leverage communication skills and connections. Individual contributors, managers and leaders alike should strive for an executive presence unique to them. You don't have to be an executive to have executive presence.

Leadership positions are big roles. They demand an inordinate amount of time, energy and dedication—much of which are invisible to others except family and close colleagues. Leaders are motivated by a desire to excel and a desire to lead business growth. Perks like salaries and benefits certainly play a role, but they are small payoffs for what is sacrificed. Still, leaders are compelled to make that sacrifice and companies are thankful.

It is possible to maintain balance or **work-life integration,** but realize the line between the two continues to be blurred by advances in technology and demands of businesses under stress. Maintaining a healthy balance demands strict attention. In some ways the principle of saying, "No," applies here. At some stage a leader has to learn to say, "No," to demands on their personal time. They also have to learn to delegate and hold their leaders and managers accountable for their decisions.

In **performance management** there are two types of letting go: 1) helping high performers rise in the company and refraining from selfishly holding them back to improve the performance of their current team, and 2) coaching poor performers out of the company and into careers that may be more suitable for their skill set. Both require courage and both require transparent leadership.

Many managers and leaders fail to keep their staff updated with honest feedback, which makes letting poor performers go harder than it has to be. The art of leadership in performance management is successfully framing the discussion and follow-up actions to actually improve performance. Should that fail, the art of leadership is counseling someone out of their current role to explore opportunities where they should have better odds for success.

The other type of letting go involves moving your top performers out of their roles and into other roles in the company where their skills as well as their contributions will make a bigger difference. For some leaders this can be as difficult as firing an employee. The trick to creating a talent pool for the organization is in replenishing that pool. A strong leader should be able to recruit and develop more talent. It's a scary and difficult effort, but that's all part of leadership.

CHAPTER SEVEN

POLARITIES, DICHOTOMIES AND MANAGING THE PENDULUM

In the 1960s, Ogilvy & Mather created an advertising campaign for Shell Oil that featured The Shell Answer Man. The Shell Answer Man had tips on everything from driving safety to saving fuel to solving regular household problems. He had all the answers, and when I arrived at Cisco that's who I felt like. It was almost too comfortable for me to step in and become the Cisco Services Answer Man. As with most things in life, there was a positive side and a negative side to this. On the positive, I was able to utilize everything I had ever done and learned in my career. It felt really good to be fully utilized. On the negative side, when it was time to relinquish control to let my own staff step up, it was hard to let go. There is something about being the person who everyone goes to, who has all the answers, that does an ego good. When the time came to loosen my grip, the prospect of not being the person that everyone relied upon was hard for me to face, especially after several consecutive years of making a powerful impact and leading the service organization to some big wins.

Eventually, a close colleague of mine took me by the elbow and said, "George, if you want to really become a leader as opposed to being a great general manager, you need to understand you're about the 'what' and the 'why.' Your managers should own the 'how' and the 'who,' and you should hold them accountable for the results and the decisions they make." This discussion repeated itself numerous times, some more heated than others. Eventually, I came to see that my colleague was right. We had stabilized the ship and now it was time to truly set sail. I knew to do that I had to stop being a manager, the Answer Man, and become a leader.

> *"The more you emphasize results, the more you have to allow staff freedom on the means to achieve those results. Staff can either say, 'Look, you can tell me what to do or you can tell me how to do it, but you can't tell me both. Either tell me the result you want and let me do it my way, or tell me I have to do it your way and then I'm not going to be responsible for the results.'"*
>
> —GEOFFREY MOORE, Chairman, TCG Advisors

As I ventured on this journey it became apparent to me that there is a dichotomy between leadership and management—that is, there are certain activity sets that can be neatly divided into the "what and why," and the "who and how." These dichotomies are as follows:

- Strategy versus tactics

- Delivery versus activities

- Portfolio management versus project management

- Teamwork-and-Collaboration (T&C) versus Command-and-Control (C&C)

I'm a fairly simple person. Although I know the world isn't entirely black and white, sometimes it helps me to frame it that way. In the next section we'll explore these dichotomies. A leader must not only learn the differences between these polarities, but must understand when and how to move between them, taking the best of each to forge a new and better reality.

TO BE OR NOT TO BE

The business world lives on a pendulum, with the focus swinging between strategy and tactics. The strategy is the what; tactics are the how. Strategy is about focus and looks into the future; tactics deal with today. Unfortunately, strategy is what business leaders persistently talk about but rarely do. Nothing frustrates me more than trying to have a strategy discussion with a leader who keeps reverting to time-tested problem solving tactics. I have ended more than one such conversation with, "If all you have to offer are tactics and you're looking to me for the answers, why do I need you?"

A healthy business can't survive on tactics or strategy alone. There has to be a balance. As Sun Tzu wrote in *The Art of War,* "Strategy without tactics is the slowest route to victory. Tactics without strategy is the noise before defeat." The difference is that whereas a company focused only on tactics may thrive for a short time and then fail, a company focused only on strategy will be lucky to survive at all.

Those who rely on tactics believe it is easier to keep doing the same thing better, faster, cheaper. Those who rely on strategy just want more time for their theories to prove out. Again, a healthy business balances strategy and tactics, with strategy informing the tactics.

Strategy takes a certain mindset to understand. I have seen more than a few well-educated professionals struggle to understand strategy. Strategy provides focus. It takes in the totality of the external environment in which a business operates, including market dynamics, competitive landscape, emerging technologies and more, as well as the internal workings of the business from finance to human resources to culture. It also takes in the syntax that binds all these factors together. It looks to the past, at the present and into the future. It establishes assumptions, sets projections, and requires rigorous analysis. Just talking about it can be exhausting. It's easy to see why leaders often times forgo strategy for "what they know is right" or for the opiate of all businesses, the implementation plan. Strategy takes a lot of effort and a lot of time to get it right.

Tactics are about accomplishing near-term goals. To deliver a goal, we build an implementation plan that plots out milestones and tasks across multiple stages. Such as an appraise stage, an execute stage, an evaluation stage and several stages in between. The implementation plan, then, is a roadmap of tactics. It can be as simple as a to-do list or as complex as a 30-page Gantt chart. As you complete the tactics in a planned and uniform way, following a carefully plotted critical path, you will eventually achieve your goals.

The key to tactics is that they should be dictated by a well thought out strategy. Unfortunately, leaders often pluck goals out of the air. "We want to be number one in customer satisfaction," for instance, is a goal. You can then underpin that goal by a series of tactics from conducting training to establishing and enforcing customer service policies, but whether that goal actually rolls up to a meaningful strategy is another question.

A great implementation plan is likely to miss big picture issues such as the competitive landscape, macroeconomics or the regulatory outlook. As an example, Larry Bossidy notes in his book, *The Discipline of Getting Things Done* that for many years General Electric was all about execution. The culture of execution was modeled by Jack Welch, emulated by leadership, and lived by the organization right down to the shop floor. The ability of Jack Welch and his leadership team to embed a culture of execution was powerful and rightfully applauded. Companies all over the world still today are trying to replicate the GE approach. The GE model, as a case study, demonstrates the influence a leader can have on an organization. Welch was all about execution and GE became all about execution. The problem here is a matter of displacement. In focusing on execution, strategy was displaced.

Bossidy states the missing element in GE's execution formulas was the people factor. I would argue that the people factor is rarely present in any execution formula, at least not in a healthy way. People factors show up in strategy. Whether businesses are publicly traded or privately owned, they are made up of people, diverse people. All this is not to say that the GE model was wrong or that it yielded bad results, my point is the people element may not have been overlooked had there been a more strategic approach.

COFFEE'S FOR CLOSERS

Everyone knows the 80/20 rule. The idea is, 20% of any activity delivers 80% of the value. A similar but more powerful ratio is the 85/15 rule. The 85/15 rule states that 85% of a team's energy is normally spent on activities, while the last 15% should be spent on delivery. The problem is, businesses usually do the first 85% incredibly well but the minute they see the goal line, they start to look at all the other bright, shiny objects and never complete the last 15%, where delivery excellence lives. In terms of the art and the science, activity is the science and delivery is the art.

In the services business, when a service is sold it takes time to deliver. Many salespeople believe when a contract is signed, the selling is done. The truth is the first 85% has been finished, but the real completion comes in delivering the services the customer paid for to the customer's satisfaction. The definition of a delivery is not your perception of what you delivered to the customer, but rather it is the customer's perception of what they received, that's the last 15%. When I had the heart-to-heart customer meeting with Bill (in Chapter Three), I was told in no uncertain terms that our company had failed to deliver that last 15%. We might have been masters of the first 85%, but without the final 15% we were nothing in our customer's eyes.

The 1992 movie *Glengarry Glen Ross* dramatized some of the worst parts of selling. The seminal moment is when Blake, played by a young Alec Baldwin, starts a fire and brimstone sales meeting by accosting a salesperson as he pours himself a cup of coffee.

Blake: "Put. That. Coffee. Down."

Salesperson: (Confused look)

Blake: "Coffee's for closers only."

In the middle of the tirade that follows, Blake spins a blackboard around and points out the A-B-C written on the board. "A-Always, B-Be, C-Closing. Always be closing, always be closing," he shouts.

What Blake is driving at is that activity without delivery is worthless. This premise may be philosophically flawed, and his leadership style suspect, but the sentiment is right—**Delivery trumps activity.** To distinguish yourself as a leader, you need to ensure your management team remembers and plans for the 15% as well as the 85%. It takes end-to-end thinking (the full 100%) and requires having the right accountabilities set with your management. Most organizations do not have the patience to take an end-to-end, concept-to-customer implementation plan and then build out an execution plan that flows from day 1 to day 2 and then onward to day 365. Failure to execute the last 15% results in lost revenues due to poor customer satisfaction and higher costs from longer rollout periods. Both will eventually expose a business to the competition.

I remember an instance in which a Cisco account team decided to bid on what looked like a large, lucrative deal. The problem was, the solution was something Cisco had never done before. A history of wins along with a "dive and catch" attitude had inflated the team's ego. They sincerely believed they could always find a way to win and let someone else deliver. Over the next seven months, the team developed out-of-the-box, creative offerings that met the customer's Request for Proposal (RFP) requirements. As one would imagine, this took an exorbitant amount of effort. At the same time the team was expending an equal amount of energy navigating internal roadblocks and obstacles that kept popping up because Cisco had never delivered a solution like this before.

After nine months of selling time, the team came to a roadblock they just could not clear. As Cisco was only a legal entity in eight of the 75 countries required to transact a managed service, the deal unraveled. The team flew into execution mode, failing to see up front that the last 15% was not even possible.

As I have noted before, sometimes you have to learn how to lose in order to learn how to win. Fast forward to a year later, the same account team won a similar piece of business for a managed TelePresence utility solution which Cisco could actually deliver under all the terms of the RFP. The deal was worth over $300 million in products and services. In this second instance the team not only planned for the 85% but the last 15% as well. In the planning they analyzed the feasibility. That win could not have been possible without the lesson from the previous loss.

Circling back to our discussion on the difference between leadership and management, it is the leader's responsibility to bring in the managers or develop the existing ones who will be able to develop a full end-to-end plan, from activity through delivery.

ONE WAY OR ANOTHER

Project management and portfolio management are often confused. Most people think project management and portfolio management are synonymous, but they aren't. The Project Management Body of Knowledge (PMBOK) defines project management as "the application of knowledge, skills, tools and techniques to project activities to meet project requirements . . . it involves planning, organizing, monitoring and controlling the project activities in order to accomplish the project requirements." PMBOK defines a portfolio as a "collection of projects or programs and other work that are grouped together to facilitate effective management of that work to meet strategic business objectives." Portfolio management is "the centralized management of one or more portfolios, which includes identifying, prioritizing, authorizing, managing, and controlling projects, programs, and other related work, to achieve specific strategic business objectives."

In simple terms, project management is about tasks, and portfolio management is about everything an enterprise does. Portfolio management is actually the first step in determining what the business should project manage. Project management is the responsibility of managers; portfolio management is the responsibility of leaders.

I recall going to meetings and being asked to make commitments on rolling out a new shared support offering across the U.S. Knowing the crucial 15% of the plan had not been laid, I had to understand if I had the resources to cover the commitment. Think of that '69 Chevelle SS 396 with 375 horsepower that I so love. If I was already using all 375 horses and somebody asked me to commit another 15, then something would have to give. In business that means we go through a prioritization process to determine what stays and what gets dropped, or at least deferred until more capacity comes on line. As part of that process, implications and risks have to be weighed to make informed decisions. The prioritization process and the decisions that flow from it are all part of portfolio management.

Every good corporation should exercise portfolio management, so when they declare there are 10 top initiatives, the organization (and customers and shareholders) can believe someone has gone through a prioritization process to weigh the benefits, risks, implications and to determine the resources needed to get those 10 initiatives done. The consequence of not exercising robust portfolio management is mass confusion. There will be a hundred different number one priorities all vying for the same attention and resources. Prioritization becomes impossible. The organization will be unable to plan or execute effectively, customers and key stakeholders will be left in the lurch and eventually the shareholders will flee.

Now, just because leadership practices portfolio management doesn't "auto-magically" guarantee success. To be successful, portfolio management requires the implicit cooperation of all leaders in an organization and strong communication to managers and staff. This leads us into our next dichotomy: teamwork-and-collaboration versus command-and-control.

Leaders get to where they are because at one time or another they solved a very hard problem. The problem may have been turning profits around, creating a track record of performance, reducing costs, or introducing innovations. Solving problems is reinforced with adulation, compensation and promotions. But any strength carried too far becomes a weakness. In many cases a manager, when presented with a problem, simply falls into their trained response. Leaders need to break the cycle of their trained responses. Remember, what got you there as a manager won't get you there as a leader. In fact, what got you there as a manager could very well kill you as a leader.

THE POWER OF "AND"

There is a time and place for both command-and-control (C&C) **and** teamwork-and-collaboration (T&C) styles of leadership. The trick is not being trapped in either style, but being able to fluidly move from one side to the other. The key skills are communication **and** connection, which are usually overlooked and underdeveloped because they are "soft skills."

First, let's get a feel for what each of these styles and cultures looks like. I say cultures because as a leadership style is fostered by more and more leaders and managers in an organization, the culture of the organization will begin to shift. The smaller the organization, the quicker and easier this will happen. In larger organizations it takes much more time and effort to tip the balance from one culture to another, though there are certainly many gradients between cultures.

Command-and-Control

So what does a C&C culture look like? A C&C culture is one in which leadership or management say with absolute authority how things will be and expects the organization to fall in line to implement. Those expectations are reinforced with policies, standards and other protocols.

The toxic aspect of a C&C culture is **dependence**. In a C&C culture the staff fall into a habit of needing to be told what to do. Surprisingly many people actually like this mode of behavior because it absolves them of responsibility. If a project turns out poorly, staff can say, "I was just doing what I was told." Management can then look at leadership and say the same thing. Leadership can either take the responsibility or, is often the case, can push it back on the organization and blame it on poor execution. The point is that if a leader wants to exercise a command-and-control style then he or she has to be accountable. A leader can't give commands and expect someone else to be accountable.

Another deadly aspect of a C&C culture is atrophy of innovation. In an environment of upward dependence, the individual and collective creative power of the wider organization is starved. Not only is the organization absolved of being accountable for any results beyond execution, they are absolved of having to think. There is nothing more dangerous than an organization that has learned to rely on their leaders to do the thinking for them.

One positive characteristic of a C&C culture is alignment. A functioning C&C culture moves in one direction and tends to be nimble and can methodically solve tactical problems to deliver results. The operative word here is "functioning." C&C culture tends to be more successful with smaller companies than larger ones. In a small organization there is less to foul up the functionality of the C&C engine—that is, there are fewer people, and hence less opportunity to cause misalignment. In short, there are less people to disagree. This explains, to some degree, the success of many startups. In a startup there is typically a small team of people to execute and one CEO or owner who is accountable for plotting out the strategy and plan.

In a large organization, a lot can go wrong in a C&C culture simply because there are more people to cause more misdirection and more leaders to spread accountability. The adage, "when everyone is responsible, no one is responsible" holds true.

Most large companies operating under a C&C leadership eventually fall into an organizational passive/aggressive dysfunction. We have all experienced the phenomenon of sitting in a meeting, coming to an agreement on a decision and then having every person do something different. Be wary of non-fatal support. Some leaders will agree to anything that does not have an outcome that would be fatal to their organization/initiative. Although this may look like alignment, it is a special kind of passive/aggressive behavior much akin to apathy. Having true alignment means all leaders are engaged and enrolled in decisions, even when it will not affect them directly. Leaders fail to understand that 75% of people will dismiss an idea out of hand regardless of the logic or veracity of the claim. Leaders fool themselves into believing that their staff is falling in line simply because the leader told them to do so and those closest to the leader tell them everything is all right.

Teamwork-and-Collaboration

Teamwork involves people working together to achieve a common goal. Inherent in this definition is cooperation and trust. Collaboration involves synthesizing knowledge and experiences from different perspectives to build better solutions. As an outcome, innovative possibilities and creative solutions are discovered which may never have been revealed otherwise.

> *"The instant a leader offers an opinion or even a suggestion to their team, they relieve their teams of accountability. Leaders often fall into this trap.*
>
> *If you want to be a strong leader, let the troops manage the business, even when they ask you to do it for them. The irony is that while everyone acknowledges they learn and grow from their mistakes, managers find it near impossible to allow their people to make their own mistakes. Many people want to be told what to do and "managers" are normally more than happy to step into that role."*
>
> —CRAIG NAKAMURA, CTO, Cisco Services US & Canada

An advantage to working in a T&C environment is that more diverse voices are heard. Working on the premise that every team member has a unique set of capabilities, the more voices heard increases the potential of high value outputs from the team. In a high-functioning T&C workplace, team members are more motivated, outputs are more valuable and resources are more evenly utilized because everyone is willing to have a stake in the game. In a perfect world, T&C clips along smoothly and everyone works for the betterment of the collective.

In reality, T&C cultures take a tremendous amount of effort and a lot can go wrong. To mitigate that risk, a T&C culture needs to be carefully nurtured.

If you are a C&C leader, results are everything; if you are a T&C leader, developing talent is everything. In business, results trump development. What happens in many companies trying to shift from C&C to T&C is that leaders try T&C for a time, but if results don't happen soon enough, it's a race right back to C&C. To win in the T&C game you need patience and a tolerance for failure. Unfortunately, patience is an anathema in business and failure is unacceptable.

TIMING IS EVERYTHING

The question of which model is better, command-and-control or collaboration and teamwork, does not have an either/or answer. The answer is both. The best leadership model is one that utilizes C&C and T&C. The art is understanding when and how to practice each.

During my tenure at Cisco, John Chambers wanted to create a simple mantra in an attempt to infuse systematic processes into the "dive and catch" culture Cisco thrived upon. To meet this need, Cisco developed a program known as Vision, Strategy and Execution (VSE). Vision was the team's shared goal over three to five years, strategy was the prioritization and alignment of resources to drive sustainable differentiation over the next one to two years, and execution was how the team would be held accountable for delivery. (Metrics were formally added to the equation after several years of implementing VSE though it was originally embedded within execution.)

Though there were many pockets of excellence coming from implementing VSE, at that stage in Cisco's evolution several things made the VSE process difficult to implement consistently.

- After **Vision,** alignment among executives, boards and councils was difficult to achieve because of an impasse between those who favored a command-and-control approach and those who favored teamwork and collaboration. This is often the case with large organizations. Cisco at the time had 70,000 employees and 25,000 contractors. Trying to align senior stakeholders with different leadership styles in such a large population is extremely difficult.

- **Strategy** was inadvertently mobilized as an execution plan aimed at solving a problem to satisfy short-term needs. As a company that prides itself on getting things done, the organization defaulted to what they did best—getting into action and solving problems.

- **Execution,** initially, lacked real-time metrics with accountabilities tied to a single leader. This was a byproduct of the teamwork-and-collaboration process. In trying to exemplify good social behavior, accountability was shared by a board or council. Also, as a product of the ambiguity within teamwork-and-collaboration geographic regions and business units were allowed to execute in ways that were suitable to them rather than leveraging standardized/centralized processes and systems. In an effort to respect local differences, inefficiencies and ambiguities were allowed to multiply.

To some extent what happened at Cisco was the opposite of what happened at GE. In Cisco's case there was a strategy, but it was outweighed by a predominant C&C culture. Without strong alignment, the culture could not be shifted enough to change the course of the overall company. The key is balancing strategy with tactics as well as balancing command-and-control with teamwork-and-collaboration. It's easy to have both strategy and tactics; the hard part is underpinning command-and-control with teamwork-and-collaboration. That takes real Chicago style friggin' magic—or a crisis.

*Know when to leverage C&C **and** when to transition to T&C. **Collaboration** should be used to develop vision and strategy, **command** in deciding objectives and direction, **teamwork** in moving forward as a unified front and **control** to execute consistently. As in sports, in business timing is everything.*

A unique challenge Cisco had as they tried to fuse C&C with T&C was in counteracting the inertia of linearity. The power of this inertia was felt when the company tried to make change happen across the entire organization while at the same time everyone was geared to deliver results to the market and shareholders every 13 weeks. In business it's a law of nature that a constant drive of linearity diminishes the organization's ability to change. The missing "X" factor in Cisco's VSE was the human factor of cultural alignment. Under the constant pressure to deliver every 13 weeks, there simply wasn't enough energy left to take on board a new strategy.

I discovered the need for alignment while creating the vision for my team. I mean real alignment, not a set of feel good slides. Once there is complete alignment on vision, the strategy has to be grounded with an agreed upon plan, preferably a project plan. Only after that should the organization be moved into execution. In practicing teamwork there is a point where each team member agrees to "opt in" for the better of the team as a whole. Teamwork can't exist where individual members tacitly "opt in" but through their actions "opt out." In true teamwork, the ego goes in the back pocket. As Randy Pond, EVP of Operations, Process and Systems at Cisco, once said: "You need to leverage teamwork-and-collaboration during the vision and strategy activities. Once you get into execution you can shift into command-and-control." He was absolutely right.

I would add that even then command-and-control should only be leveraged if it is strategically called for. For example, command-and-control works in non-complex linear business environments where the external and internal drivers are two-dimensional and predictable, decisions need to be made quickly and corrective steering can have immediate effect. In these environments many organizations can get bogged down, throwing flowers at the altar of consensus. Conversely, command-and-control is never good in a highly complex matrix environment when a single track drive can land you in the wrong place very quickly with little chance for recovery.

INSTANT REPLAY

A great manager is a master of the "how" and the "who." A great manager owns implementation and knows how to leverage resources to make sure projects, initiatives and activities are executed on time and on budget. A strong leader, on the other hand, is a master of the "what" and the "why": What needs to be done and why it needs to be done. The "how" and the "who" are in service of the "what" and the "why." Leadership decides the "what" and the "why" and then empowers management to determine the "how" and the "who." There's a lot of detail and work that goes into each role, but they are both necessary, and they are both distinct.

As leaders, we need to stretch ourselves out farther than where our teams are. Before I could take my services sales organization through transformation, I had to stop being a manager and become a leader. It was only then that I could be a role model and coach others through transformation. As leaders we need to have the courage to give our own managers the choice to be leaders or to just sit back and say, "Tell me what to do coach."

To become an effective leader we need to come to terms with the dichotomies of leadership, so we can effectively move back and forth from each side of the mirror, leveraging the strengths of each for the benefit of the customer, the organization and the shareholders.

Strategy provides long-term focus informed by internal culture and external marketing conditions. Tactics provide the means to implement a strategy in the here and now. High-performing organizations balance tactics and strategy. We would be hard-pressed to find a leader who does not understand the importance of having both strategy and tactics in an organization. It's management 101. On the other hand, finding a leader that can work in both spheres is rare indeed. Many start with the best of intentions—articulating a compelling vision, having a clear mission—but fail to join it up in a full strategy. They simply jump into their most comfortable space—problem solving via tactics.

Organizations can get so wrapped up in activities they forget about the last 15%—delivery. Delivery is the most important thing for the customer. It's what they pay for, it's what they expect. The customer could not care less for the first 85%; it is the delivery they are waiting on. Strategy, and the portfolios that underpin them, need to be planned and delivered end-to-end and then measured by customer satisfaction. Consistently following through to the point of delivery will secure customer loyalty and do more for sustaining a business than an entire career of dive and catch saves.

The ability to plan, manage and execute projects is a mark of a good company. The ability to manage a portfolio is the mark of a great company. Portfolio management isn't just a program office that oversees multiple projects; rather, it enables leadership with the capability to prioritize objectives, make decisions, manage and mitigate risks and control resources to attain a company's strategic objectives. Leaders sometimes confuse the sequencing of activities as portfolio management. Portfolio management not only involves choices about which priorities are top tier and lower tier, but what is core and what is context and how much of the context should actually be taken off the table.

There is nothing inherently wrong with a C&C leadership style. In non-complex, linear markets, C&C can be quite effective. It also tends to be effective in small start-ups. The larger the organization and the more complex the market, the more can go wrong in a C&C organization. T&C leadership is extremely difficult to maintain as well. The unruly aspect of T&C is cooperation. An organization operating with a T&C can be ambiguous, slow to action and lack direction.

In the 1993 sci-fi thriller, *Jurassic Park,* there's a scene when one of the children, Tim, picks up a pair of night vision goggles. Donald Gennara, the lawyer, looks at him and asks, "Are they heavy?"

Tim nods yes.

Donald responds, "Then they're expensive, put 'em down."

My journey over the years has led me to the conclusion that moving an organization to a hybrid culture of T&C and C&C is a heavy object to lift but it is absolutely worth the effort. In section four we will explore transforming organizations more thoroughly, since we all have leadership blind spots.

The temptation is always going to be there to stay on the science side of the leadership mirror and manage an organization through C&C. Resist the temptation. The reality is that there are instances in which C&C is necessary, but you must have the courage to step into T&C and allow your team to make decisions, manage the business and to be held accountable. That's what the art of leadership is all about.

TRANSFORMING AN ORGANIZATION

*"The growth and development of people
is the highest calling of leadership."*

—HARVEY FIRESTONE

CHAPTER EIGHT

JOB ONE

Too many leaders focus too much time on trying to create value solely through financial and commercial levers. Sustainable value in business comes through people. The first step to creating value through people is by hiring, developing and retaining the right talent. This threefold mission should be "job one" for any leader in business. The problem is that since so many leaders are steeped in the science of the leadership, they naturally approach this mission with limited success. The science of hiring, development and retention looks like this:

- With a scientific angle to **hiring** we assess technical skills and determine how well a candidate will be able to perform in the future based on previous experiences and current skill sets.

- In **development,** the scientific approach leverages formal training to sharpen technical skills, which are good for us as managers. Improving soft skills such as communication, influence management, executive presence, is seen as nice to have but not necessary.

- In **retention,** science focuses on rewards, especially monetary and material, which people love to receive but, unfortunately, the staying power of these rewards is short-lived. Often monetary and material rewards create inflationary pay for performance expectations.

The principles and practices we will examine in this chapter take us to the other side of the mirror, to the art side, the customer's side. Specifically, I'll share hiring and interviewing techniques that have helped me to understand the inherent leadership skills and internal drivers of potential employees. I will also share some valuable lessons and tools I learned from The Liberty Consulting Team that I used to help my Cisco leadership team and myself to develop as individuals and as a team. We'll also look at ways to improve retention.

EVERY WHICH WAY

The feature that most distinguishes today's employees from previous generations is the level of loyalty people have, or rather don't have, to their employers. This is especially true with employees from generations X and Y, though it is true of some baby boomers as well. For example, once in a job for 18 to 24 months, today's employee will take account of how they are "tracking" within the organization. They want to know "what is in this for them." If they don't feel they are progressing quickly enough, if they have a line on a better opportunity somewhere else, and especially if they have a friend already in the other company, they won't hesitate to turn in their two-week's notice and follow the new opportunity. Despite the economy, or maybe because of the economy, many employees feel what is best for them trumps what is best for the company. There is nothing wrong with this attitude, but leaders need to know it exists and need to have an appropriate strategy for dealing with it.

Today, people are using a new set of rules for managing their careers more effectively. People see the value in gathering varied experiences garnered from working for multiple companies. Career progression has morphed from the traditional vertical to the decidedly diagonal. In the past people would have to wait their turn to move up in a company. Nowadays if there is a perceived bottleneck, people are more than willing to step sideways and move up—that is, they move diagonally.

For some reason many companies value the skills of external candidates more highly than internal candidates. It is a classic case of the devil you know versus the devil you don't know. The bias is that external candidates have a wider range of experience and bring into the organization new and divergent perspectives. A side effect of this phenomenon is it is often easier to "climb the ladder" if you leave a company than try to move up within one company. Many people have learned that by exiting the box you can re-enter it at a higher level.

> *"We're going from a product-centric, technology-led business to a solutions and services-led business. My worry is, 'Do we have the talent to execute against that plan?' Because it all starts with our people and the skills that our people have, and so how we recruit them, how we get them engaged, how we develop them, and how we retain them is critical."*
>
> —JERE BROWN, CEO, Americas, Dimension Data

Another aspect of today's employment landscape is the increasing number of contract employees. More and more companies are contracting out work they used to do internally in an effort to decrease labor costs and increase access to a wider and deeper range of expertise. At its zenith of employee head count, Cisco had over 70,000 direct employees and another 25,000+ contractors. The theory was for core work and activities to be done by direct employees while context work was delivered by contractors.

At one time contract work was seen as a stigma. Being a contractor suggested that the person didn't have what it took to be a "badged" employee. Today as employees seek more creative work and new opportunities, contract work is used as a means to "test drive" a diverse slate of companies and to be more selective in deciding which company, if any, to pursue for long-term employment. Contract work to hire becomes a win–win solution for both the employee and employer as each gets to try the other out before making a direct employee commitment.

With fewer and fewer employees willing to work in hierarchical companies the implications are multifold. For one, candidates may be less willing to wait before taking another offer. Additionally, more and more candidates actually prefer working as contractors where their obligations to the company leave them less constrained. Another impact is the type of benefits a company may offer to attract potential staff—for instance, long-term incentives like 401Ks have less influence than in the past. Even start-ups today are having a hard time attracting and retaining employees since the dream of making it big with stock options has clearly diminished.

On the flip side, I have seen people stay at companies far too long, not because of how great the company is or all the opportunities for advancement, but because they like their manager or leader. While this may seem like a benefit for the company, stagnant talent is never a good thing.

A strong leader will check in with his or her team members to find out why they are in their role and where they want to go next. If they are in the role for the same reasons when they first joined the team, it can be a sign they are overly loyal to you as a leader. As a leader it's your job to ensure your staff are growing in their careers and continuing to build their capabilities. This is not easy to acknowledge because having an "All Pro" seasoned team is wonderful, but as a leader you are accountable for their continued development, which benefits the employee as well as the company.

> *"The biggest challenge that I have is attracting and retaining the very best talent. The better they get, the faster they want to keep moving. So my effort is to attract, motivate and retain the very best talent and keep them energized and refreshed because not everybody can be a four-star general."*
>
> —WOODY SESSOMS, SVP, Global Enterprise, Cisco Systems

Employees need to own their career and leaders need to own helping them progress. The options are fairly straight-forward: you can fail to develop staff and everyone loses, you can develop their technical skills and hold them in place, in which case you win and the employee loses, or you can invest in developing your staff's technical as well as their life skills, and everyone wins.

Leaders need to break down the barriers to help people move up diagonally inside their own companies. If done creatively and consistently, a company's culture will flourish and become more successful.

LOG IN, SIGN UP

Social networks are having a marked impact on the employee market. It used to be when someone hired on to a business, it was just that one employee. Today it's them plus their extended social network of friends held together by Twitter, Facebook, LinkedIn, Pinterest, Tagged, MySpace, myYearbook, Google+, Yahoo! Answers and more. As they check into their personal network during breaks, over lunch or at home, they may be inclined to share with their entire online social network just how great or terrible their boss is or how wonderful or awful it is to work at XYZ company. The range and extent of this network is called "social reach." Every employee has social reach and every employer is subject to it.

The adage "always be recruiting" is as true today as it was yesterday. In addition to the tried and true face-to-face methods, like networking at conferences or social events, social media can play an important role in attracting talent.

Just as negative impressions can race through a matrix of thousands in matter of seconds, so can positive impressions. If you have a few hundred contacts on Facebook or LinkedIn, how many people within 24 hours do you think would see a status change or a job opening you posted? How many people if your employer branding is strong? The point is the potential to open the recruiting floodgates is astoundingly simple today.

My connection in LinkedIn alone has a social reach of over 11 million professionals. Here is how it works:

- Primary connections: In LinkedIn at the time of this writing, I have 2,500+ friends and colleagues.

- Secondary connections: Two degrees away I have over 410,000 connections. These are friends of friends.

- Tertiary connections: Three degrees away I have over 11,451,305 potential contacts. These are friends and contacts of my secondary connections.

Adding my primary, secondary, and tertiary connections, I have over 11,863,805 potential contacts. Now add to that number the contacts I can make through other media channels such as Twitter and Facebook and the number is truly astronomical.

As many people and companies have discovered, there is a dark side to social networks. Surprisingly, what can be more damaging to a company's culture and brand is not the disgruntled employee who leaves, it is the disgruntled employee who stays. Consider both of these scenarios—the disgruntled employee who leaves and the one that stays. In both cases, they reach out to their social network and tell everyone what a bad experience they had with the company and, in some cases, their manager. Those details and the impact they carry spread across their social reach with astounding speed. That speed, which initiates within milliseconds and can last for years, is called "share velocity."

The difference with the disgruntled employee who stays on is they perpetuate their poison with fresh barrages fueled by new experiences day after day and month after month—until they finally do leave. One disgruntled employee today can equal thousands of negative impressions on your brand with astounding share velocity. For the unhappy employee that stays on, multiply that by the number of days they stay on, or worse, the number of times they log on each day.

EVERY CANDIDATE GETS A VOTE

Many employers believe the ball is in their hands once an individual is brought through the recruiting pipeline and they begin the interview process, effectively advancing from prospect to candidate. The reality is not just that the interviewer scrutinizes candidate, but the candidate scrutinizes the interviewer and the company he or she represents. Unlike politics, the candidate gets a vote, too.

As my dad used to tell me, "Kid, in selling as in life, you never have a second chance to make a first impression." When a candidate walks into your company's lobby, as they walk the hallways passing cubes and offices, and then eventually as they exit the building, they are doing something most people miss—they are looking for people who look like them. If they are young Hispanics, they will look for other young Hispanics; if they are sports enthusiasts, they will look for telltale signs of other enthusiasts; if they are experienced hires, they will keep an eye out for other business veterans. Affinity, as they say, governs proximity—that is people want to be where they feel welcomed.

In addition, potential employees are keeping an eye out for signs about the company's culture. For instance, they may read cultural significance into how many people are eating at their desks, suggesting how pressured staff are under to produce; what type of pictures and decorations, if any, people have on display, indicating how open and accepting the employer and other staff are to their lifestyles; the amount of employees engaged in friendly chatter; the number of people marching or storming down halls; the number of cars in the parking lot after 5:00 PM. People used to make decisions about joining a company based on the reputation of the company, the quality of job, who they would work for and, of course, salary. Today even if these factors say "yes," but the culture says "no" the candidate is likely to walk. Leaders need to understand that this silent but critical evaluation happens every day. As leaders, we need to be aware that the radar is always on before the defense shields go up.

Perception is the silent killer. You need to know how you, your company, your products, or services are perceived. Take time to step back and read your office to see what visitors may perceive about your company's diversity and culture.

MAGIC EIGHT BALL

In the 70s, there was a novelty toy called the Magic Eight Ball. They are still around today and have a whole variety of spin offs like the Psychotherapy Ball or, my favorite, the Affirmation Ball. The way the Magic Eight Ball works is you ask it a yes-no question and then turn the ball over to reveal the answer, which is inscribed on a 20-sided die floating within the ball itself. The answers range from affirmative to negative to non-committal responses. So you could ask the ball if you should go out to eat tonight or if you should get married tomorrow and it would provide you with an answer.

I always thought a fortune could be made if someone could create a "magic interview ball" that would tell you everything you needed to know about a job candidate. Barring the invention of such a device anytime soon, I will instead offer tips on interviewing, including questions that I developed from years of hiring successes and mistakes.

The first principle I use in interviewing is to delve for indications of strong self-awareness. The more a candidate knows his or her own strengths and weaknesses, their mistakes and accomplishments, the better leader the person is likely to be. I am convinced a person cannot effectively lead others unless they understand their motivations, faults, and fears. I am also convinced people will not follow someone they think is disingenuous, at least not for long.

The second principle I use in the interview process is to look at their potential future performance based on internal drivers instead of looking backward at past performance-based technical skills.

With these two guiding principles, I then use several key questions to get to the insights I need to help me make a good hiring decision. Here are the topics upon which I base my "magic questions." I do not necessarily delve into them all during any single interview, but rather I make a choice depending on the flow of the interview.

1. **Juggling:** Like a good juggler, an important skill managers and leaders need is the ability to keep all the balls in the air. In juggling priorities, everyone will drop a few balls. The question is, which ones will they drop and why? I probe into this area to determine how they prioritize and how they react to the reality of "you can't do it all." Do they overwork themselves, beat themselves up, delegate, or look for smarter ways to do things? You can also apply this theory once you have hired a candidate by giving them multiple activities and deliverables to accomplish over a short period and then see which ones they drop. You know they will not keep them all in the air. Your interest, again, is which ones they drop and why.

2. **Matrices:** I often ask candidates how they work in a matrix organization. I prompt for specific examples about how they deal with ambiguity and lack of formal control, how they influence without authority while at the same time being held accountable for delivering substantial results. Even if your company is not a matrix organization, the ability to effectively navigate through a matrix of customers, suppliers and partners is crucial for a strong leader. Some classic scenario questions are: Give me an example of time when you were responsible for delivering a result but could only

influence the key players. How did you learn that skill? What was the outcome, and what did you do differently as a result? My caution is, beware of leaders and managers who require direct reporting relations in order to deliver results.

3. **Role model:** Another question I find revealing is, "Do you have a role model, personal or professional?" On the surface, the question seems common and predictable—similar to "who's your hero." The genuine answer comes with a degree of awkwardness because to sincerely answer this question takes a willingness to be vulnerable. The question is really about being brave enough to be vulnerable for moment. If they are willing to be vulnerable in an interview, chances are they will be vulnerable with their staff. A willingness to be vulnerable is part of the secret sauce of building relationships.

4. **Influences:** A question more specific to sales but which can easily be modified for other disciplines is, "Where did you learn how to sell?" Early in our careers, most of us are eager to learn, eager to please and very impressionable. We do our best to emulate those we admire. Consciously or subconsciously, those early lessons tend to stick with us and bubble up later in life. As sociologist Dr. Morris Massey has so well articulated in his *What You Are Is Where You Were When* video, "Don't let a past you can't change write your future script." Think for a moment about your first or second manager and what they taught you. Chances are what that person taught you back then will closely resemble who you are today. It is not that we stop growing, but as with children, it is during those formative, indelible years that we are stamped with lasting lessons and memories. For instance, if your most influential manager (generally your first one) taught you to be skeptical of data assumptions, as a leader you will likely question the underlying assumptions of every solution presented you. Another way to get this kind of insight is to leverage preference and personality assessment tools. Using one of the many tools available, for instance, may classify the above noted "skeptical of data assumptions" characteristic as a "high verifier."

5. **Talents:** At times, I will ask the question, "God blesses everybody with a special talent, skill, or ability. What's your special sauce, what makes you unique?" This question is about diversity—not about the symbols of

diversity such as race, religion, color—but about differences. The response to this question is always interesting and again, with some vulnerability, candidates will show what they think is truly special about themselves. People sometimes feel they do not really have a special talent that sets them apart. The reality is, however, that something they think is "ordinary" may in fact be "extraordinary." I have said before that a company could be exponentially more effective if "they only knew what they know." Finding out what people know, understanding their differences, and hence strengths, begins in the interview process. Imagine the possibilities of how you could leverage the strengths of your team if you knew their special talents.

6. **Mistakes:** I also try to understand how well the person takes responsibility for their mistakes. The question is straightforward, "Tell me about the biggest mistake you've made?" Here again, I am looking for a real discussion on what they learned from it and how they handled it.

In 1966, Julian Rotter proposed that people are guided either by an internal or an external sense of control. Those guided by an internal locus of control feel the circumstances of life around them can be deeply influenced by their actions; those with an external locus of control feel life is out of their control.[7] This theory became popular with human resource professionals in the 1990s as a key value to look for in employees. Internal locus of control indicated an employee would take accountability for their actions and drive for improvement. You want those folks on your team. Asking people about their biggest mistake will give you a direct line to identifying their locus of control.

7. **People:** Another situation-based question I ask is how candidates have invested in developing others and/or themselves. The answer could be anywhere from formal learning and development to informal mentoring and coaching. What I am looking for is an indication about how they see people development as contributing to the success of an enterprise. For my money, personal coaching and mentoring beat out classroom training any

---

[7] Julian Rotter's original assessment and many updated variations of it can easily be found online.

day. I would rather hear about a candidate's experience of being a role model for their staff than hear a list of courses or conferences they attended.

A good follow-up question is whether they have had 360-degree feedback and what they learned from it. 360-degree feedback, or multisource feedback, is drawn from people who work with an employee at all levels, such as their managers and peers as well as those who report to them. It also includes a self-assessment. In some cases, it may involve input from external sources like customers and suppliers. I like to ask what actions they took to improve themselves based on the feedback they received.

8. **Leisure:** It may sound simple, but what a person does in their spare time is important. Asking questions in this area allows me to get a view into what makes a candidate tick, which in turn tells me what kind of leader they are likely to be. Are they a 7/24 Type A personality, do they relax by engaging in complex activities, do they drive for expertise outside of the workplace, are they open to new experiences? There are no right or wrong answers to this question.

9. **The biggies:** My favorite questions are: "If money were no object, what would you be doing tomorrow?" and "If you worked at our organization for the next ten years and it was time for you to cash in and drive off into the sunset, what would you want your legacy to be?" I always ask at least one of these questions during an interview with a candidate that I think has half a chance at the role.

This I know: people who answer these two questions the quickest are the ones who may lack good insight into themselves. A genuine answer will come with some hesitation, a lot of looking up to the right (where people tend to gaze when they are being introspective), and usually a change in the tone of voice, connoting emotion and vulnerability. These are questions you want people to chew on. Unless you have spent a lot of money on therapy or lived in a monastery, it is hard to fake answers to these questions, especially the second. I have conducted over 50 interviews in the last several years and out of those 50 interviews, less than five people answered either of these questions quickly and, at the same time, well.

This is a short-list of my favorite questions. Again, it is not so much about the actual questions so much as what the questions and subsequent discussion help to reveal. As with any endeavor, there is always more than one way to arrive at the prize.

As a quick aside, I will share the one question I used to ask but have since stopped using. If you ask someone to tell you about their communication style, they will always say, "It's direct." I have never heard anyone say, "Well, I've got a kind of a mealy-mouth, you know, talk-out-of-the-side-of-my-mouth indirect communication style." So I learned not to ask that question, but rather to get at it a different way.

TRICK ME ONCE

Many leaders fancy themselves great interviewers and judges of talent, but few actually are. Everyone has a set of hot questions he or she asks based on how they have been burned in the past. Many people mentally phase out of an interview once their "burn" questions have been checked off either in the affirmative or negative. Have you ever been in an interview scheduled for an hour and it last about 30-40 minutes and wondered why it ended quickly? It was likely because you had given the interviewer enough answers to check off their "burn list."

The risk here, of course, is that talent may be hiding in the blinders built around the "burn list." To compensate for this tendency I rely on a team of select interviewers to vet the technical skills. That allows me the space to focus on the non-technical and behavioral indicators of leadership.

I also feel strongly about the benefits of using personality or preference assessments to help provide candidate-driven insight into areas that I may overlook. Some assessments that can be powerful indicators of leadership skills are the Myers Briggs Type Indicator (MBTI), Fundamental Interpersonal Relations Orientation (FIRO B), DiSC and Predictive Index. There are many others. Before using them be sure to research them carefully, always use a certified practitioner and consult with your human resource professional about how and when to insert them into the selection process. These tools can help uncover motivating needs, predicting, describing, and measuring the work behavior and potential of individuals and groups at all organizational levels.

If used properly, preference and personality assessments can provide visibility into the blind spots of the interviewing process.

Before we leave the topic of interviewing, here are some additional best practices:

- **Results:** My dad was fond of saying, "coaches lose ball games while players win the games." It is always a good idea to focus on "how" a person achieved a result as opposed to "what" result they achieved. It is one thing to say you improved sales and quite another to explain how you and your team actually did it. Another thing to listen for here is how often a person says "I" versus "we." If they use "I" as opposed to "we" when explaining results, they are taking the credit for themselves when they should be sharing it with their team.

- **Control:** Watch to see if and how a candidate takes control of the interview. If you are looking for a strong-willed manager, perhaps you want them to take control. For me, I look for someone with more of a collaborative style with good listening skills. If done well, a good candidate can dialogue without appearing to wrestle for dominance in the interview.

First examine the quality of the questions from the candidate, then assess if you were able to ask all of your questions, as well as answer all the candidate's questions. If yes, then you and the candidate were able to "manage" a dialogue. If no, then it may be an indicator of how the candidate will manage discussions with customers and staff.

- **Stretch:** When hiring for roles that require a lot of relationship building I look for candidates who feel they are overqualified for the job. If they are overqualified, they could spend the extra energy and time on building alliances and relationships internally with staff and externally with clients, partners, suppliers, customers.

"Assessments provide the science element in the art of the hiring. Given that selecting the right talent is the sales leader's first challenge, applying scientifically-valid assessments can take the traditionally poor hiring results from about 33% to a quantum improvement of 90%+. By accurately predicting the candidate's sales aptitude, proven tools can eliminate the mystery piece in the hiring process."

—NANCY CLARK, President, Leadership Dynamics, Inc.

Relationships trump talent all day long. If the technical aspect of the new role is a "stretch" from where they have been AND they need to build relationships, often times it is a bridge too far.

- **Succession:** One of the top issues leaders have in getting to their next level is not having someone to backfill their own role. Leaders can easily back themselves into a corner because of their hiring practices. I have observed that although people advise "A" players should hire "A+" players, it turns out "A" players usually hire "B" players. "B" players, in turn, hire "C" and "C" players hire "D" players. The point is to address this at your level or your staff's level. Do not be afraid to hire someone who may be better than you or who can do your job. You will need them so you can move on the next level. In addition, as noted earlier, strong leaders have the ability and confidence to hire, develop and promote great talent repeatedly.

- **Reverse-blinders:** Another phenomenon in hiring is the fact that most leaders hire people who are similar to themselves. After hiring in their own reflection, they rarely wake up to the reality that they are being worked by their key leaders because their team is just like them. Do not dismiss candidates who come across as completely new and different. Sometimes these candidates bring unique skill sets to the table and special differences that can take a team (and you) to the next level.

- **Perspective:** Multiple perspectives are better than one. A practice I have seen work in the favor of both the employer and the potential employee is multiple interviews. Moreover, it will not be just two or three interviews, but eight or ten or more. Cisco did this extremely well and the bigger the job, the more interviews. Though it may initially be a pain for the candidate, it pays dividends later. In fact you can say it benefits the employer upfront and the employee soon after. For the employer, it affords a better sense of who the candidate really is. Multiple perspectives will always provide a more rounded and accurate view of the candidate. For the potential employee, if they are hired they have 10 best friends on day one. A word of caution, however, if you take top candidates through 10-15 interviews AND it takes you 3-4 months to make this happen, they will lose interest in joining the company.

- **Informal.** For roles such as vice president and senior vice president, I interact with candidates in settings other than the formal interview. Candidates enjoy this because it gives them more face time and, if handled well by the employer, it can feel very non-pressured. The settings can be range anywhere from work related events such as touring the campus, to social events such as dinners, to recreational events such as golf. The same way a company's perceived culture may not match up with the company's rhetoric, so a candidate's informal behaviors may not be congruent with their formal answers.

  Over dinner, I watch for the level of conversation with which they are comfortable, their depth and breadth of current events, variety of interests and their fluidity in social interactions. On the golf course I look for whether they adhere to the rules, how easily they lose their temper and the kind of etiquette they follow. These may seem trivial but they are indicators to how well a candidate's unintentional behaviors match their intentional messages.

Interviewing will always be an inexact science. Through the magic of a few well-placed questions, you are trying to divine a person's future performance. In a way, it really is like a Magic Eight Ball, as you never really know until after the person has started and is doing the job. What many people fail to see is that core to the hiring process is what happens after a candidate is brought on board as an employee. As my father used to tell me, "Kid, you'll know at your gut level in the first 30 days whether the person's going to work out or not." He then added, "If you follow your gut and pull the trigger within the first 90 days, you can say you made a bad decision and took the necessary actions to fix it. If you wait past 90 days and you let the person stick around for six to nine months, then it falls on you as to why you made the mistake and then put up with the mistake for that long."

Most managers and leaders will not admit they made a hiring error and will tolerate poor performance for incredible periods of time or until someone new comes in and cleans up. The bottom line is you are responsible for the hiring decisions you make. If you make a poor decision, then you need to take accountability and rectify the problem. If you make a great decision, then you need to invest in that decision and develop them just as carefully as you would if you just made a multi-million investment in the market.

 Sometimes it is better to fire the behavior and not the person.

CAN'T GET NO SATISFACTION

Since the 1980s, it has been fashionable for companies to offer quirky benefits to recruit talent, buoy morale, and retain staff. This is nowhere more evident than in California's Silicon Valley, home of Google, Facebook, Apple and other tech giants. These benefits range from car washes to pet friendly offices, massage rooms, TOTO-brand heated toilet seats, Friday afternoon beer bashes, and wine tastings.

In using benefits as a recruiting tool, I have learned that if people are too concerned about what benefits they might get, they probably are not right for the job. One would hope that a senior manager or director, for instance, would be more interested in the challenge and scope of a role rather than pet sitting options or the kinds of electronic games available in the café.

Using benefits as morale boosters and retention tools are good, as part of the overall strategy, but leaders need to differentiate benefits from entitlements. **Benefits** are short-term and are bound to events or accomplishments, whereas entitlements are indefinite in duration, and are not typically tied to an event or accomplishment. For instance, a wine tasting event for exceeding quarterly targets is a benefit; Friday afternoon beer bashes "just because" is an entitlement. Under this definition, when benefits end, people are likely to understand—especially if the linkage between the benefit and the criteria is clearly communicated. When entitlements are revoked, that is a different story. Revoking entitlements, no matter the rationale, will have negative impacts on morale. When people have something they perceive as an entitlement taken away, they feel they are being punished. The time to manage benefits and entitlements is before they are offered and not when it is time to take them away.

 Every benefit and entitlement needs an exit strategy.

 **INSTANT REPLAY**

Organizations are made up of people and as such, the success of any organization begins and ends with people. The drivers and motivations that spur people to join one organization over another and then to develop themselves and their careers have shifted over the last fifty years. Joining is more about how a job aligns with a person's lifestyle expectations and development is more about personal growth.

Underlying this has been an ongoing erosion of loyalty to the company that has been replaced by loyalty to the self. This is not an indictment of today's workforce but a simple statement of fact. In today's world of rapid consumerism, the technologies and benefits the public has grown used to in their "everyday" lives are expected to exist in their "workplace" lives as well. A leader can try to swim against that current or they can learn to swim with the current, and even leverage it to their advantage. This premise holds true with recruiting tools and benefit programs on how your culture shows up to potential candidates. For instance, I hear leaders everywhere bemoaning the advent of texting, social media, and other technologies that have displaced things like face-to-face and phone conversations. While lamenting the past has a certain romantic nostalgia, it will not get you very far in business. Rather than mourning the passing of yesterday's communication channels, I recommend embracing today's. The sheer velocity and reach of social networking can yield incredible results in the recruiting arena, both positive and negative. It also has a place in developing and retaining staff.

The things that made you famous in the past will not make you famous in the future. Knowing is key. This is especially true in the interviewing process where the effort must be on knowing who the candidates really are and how they will perform as leaders. Most managers and even leaders focus on assessing the technical skills of potential employees. While technical skills are important for most roles, it should not be up to leaders to assess those skills. A strong leader should agree on the technical competencies and capabilities they need in an employee and should make sure they have an interview panel or assessment tool that will gauge those skills. The leader should focus on assessing leadership skills, especially indicators that will point to a person's level of self-awareness.

CHAPTER NINE

GIVE ME LIBERTY OR GIVE ME DEATH

Most people who have worked in an office environment can tell you about business politics, bad behaviors, and that one borderline "psycho-employee." My question is this: Where do these behaviors, good and bad, come from and how can we improve them? I maintain that these behaviors are natural offshoots of our development process as social beings and they can become better or worse depending on the type of reinforcement we provide in the workplace. If you picked up this book looking for a leadership insight that can change the landscape of your workplace for the better, here is one insight I can offer you. You can significantly improve staff development and talent retention by raising the maturity factor of your teams.

As with so many things in life, there are two sides to this coin. One is eliminating bad behaviors; the other is enhancing good behaviors. Eliminating juvenile behaviors and dysfunction from the workplace can take the most toxic working environment and make it a place where employees feel safe, comfortable, and productive. At the same time enriching positive interactions in the workplace, improving relationship building and the maturity level of conversations also enhances the work environment.

Let us say you have taken on a new team. You have inherited some great talent and you have brought in some more. Along the way, a few people have opted out, and you took proactive measures with a few others. After several months, you now have what you consider the basis of a strong team. Congratulations, well done.

The next step is to move from an All Star team of individuals to a high performing unified team. All-star teams are very skilled individuals who come together for a meeting or project. They have the appearance of being on the same team because they all wear the same uniform, but once they leave, they go back to their own team or group. They never really become a high-performing team. They put on the all-star team uniform for that hour, day, or week, but underneath they are still loyal to their home team. To help a team grow from All Star to high performing, you will have to help your staff—and yourself—to . . . grow up.

To illustrate how this works, allow me to share with you some experiences I had leading the Cisco services sales organization. I was at a juncture with my team where I knew we needed to make some significant behavioral and cultural adjustments. I began to keep an eye out for someone who could help my team—leaders and staff alike—make the laborious transition that was before us. We needed a common lens to see ourselves and a common taxonomy to speak about what we saw. More importantly, it had to be legitimate and understandable.

In today's market, if you walk outside and throw a rock in any direction you are likely to hit someone who has a theory on people behavior they would love to sell you. Most of them are based upon academics and not really pressure tested in business. Not being a behavioral science expert, I had something of a selection dilemma on my hand. The only compass I had to go by was my personal views of organizational effectiveness formed by over 20,000 hours of practice.

My communications director at the time, Naomi Chavez-Peters, was familiar with the works and results of Larry Liberty, PhD., an organizational consultant. She felt his way of approaching organizational improvement aligned with my vision. In short order, she arranged for us to meet. While I do not think our first meeting was something you would find retold in *The Atlantic* magazine's "First Encounters" section, it did mark the beginning of a turning point for my organization and me.

GROWING PAINS

According to Larry, the normal development cycle of a human being—both physiologically and psychologically—is a transition from infancy to youth to adolescence and finally adulthood. The Liberty model suggests that by the measure of psychological development, when people enter the workplace they are psychologically and emotionally "adolescents" or "adults."

The Liberty model provides a way of assessing ourselves and seeing how psychologically and emotionally mature we are at any particular moment in time. As the workplace can be the nexus of stress, the model also provides a way of understanding what happens to us under duress. For instance, does stress make us more mature or less mature? This understanding allows us to both anticipate and predict how we will react in various circumstances, including times of change. The true value of the model comes in showing the things we need to do to optimize our maturity.

The two subcategories in the adolescents' component of the model are "low-functioning adolescents" and "high-functioning adolescents." Low-functioning adolescents are fundamentally at the bottom rung of effectiveness in our society. These are the folks you might expect to see on an episode of *The Jerry Springer Show*. They show up for their moment of fame and never grow out of that particular experience. They will be that way next week, next month, and next year.

By contrast, the high-functioning adolescent gets along very well in society when things are running smoothly. They are productive, motivated and, in the workplace particularly, inclined to periods of results-driven activity. Under stress, however, they may lose control, act out, yell, or become frustrated, flustered, and indecisive. In other cases, they may feel helpless and become prone to depression. While this may seem extreme, there are other less overt ways in which high-functioning adolescents act out such as passive/aggressive behaviors, inappropriate denial, and other obstructive conduct. None of these behaviors is what you would like to experience in the workplace.

The two stages of adult are young adult and wise adult. Young adults are adults in training, as Larry likes to call them. They have moments of being adolescents who have crossed over the maturity line into early stages of adulthood, and yet at times they may slip back into high-functioning adolescent behavior. A wise adult is the fully formed human being, someone who has learned and experienced to fully function in adulthood: examples would be Mahatma Gandhi or Colin Powell, although neither would likely call themselves such—another telltale sign that they are.

The reality is that most people are a combination of two stages. A person will rarely move wholly from one stage to another, but instead progress through different areas at different paces. In this way, the typical person is continually shifting back and forth between stages based on the stimulus they experience in the moment. For instance, when you wake up in the morning you wake up either as an adult or as an adolescent. (The wake-up state for an adolescent is usually anxiety, fear, and doubt about how the day will go. The wake-up state for an adult is gratitude and appreciation for life.) During the day, circumstances conspire for you or against you, exasperating both the adult and the adolescent.

The most distinguishable difference between adolescents and adults is the ability to manage their reactions and emotions. Anyone who has had teenagers knows about angst and mood swings based upon certain stimulus/response cycles. The reality is that while chronological adults may not look like teenagers, they can easily act like them.

"Tell me about the biggest mistake you have made in your career" is an interview question that can effectively reveal which stage of maturity the interviewee is in. A high-functioning adolescent will invariably blame the

> *"I've met a few wise adults. I've paid a lot of attention to them, I've interviewed them, I've watched them. I would estimate wise adults make up a scant 5% of the population and they hardly ever, ever, ever transgress from being a wise adult to anything less. When you get there, there's a foundation that's so deep and wide, in terms of ethics, beliefs, psychological and emotional balance, and self-insight that you, basically, you wake up in the morning and you just, basically, love your life."*
>
> —LARRY LIBERTY, PhD., The Liberty Consulting Team

mistake on anything except himself or herself, whereas the adult will take full responsibility for the decision and for the failure.

Two of the most powerful tools in helping someone progress from a lower stage of maturity to a higher one are as follows:

- **Coach and provide opportunities for self-insight.** One of the characteristics of an adult, both young and wise, is to be coachable. One of my passions is golf. In golf, virtually all the top professionals in the world have access to regular coaching and feedback. Golf is so complicated and needs such precision that when we are just a little off we cannot perform at our best. In life, the same holds true. Adults can get an edge on life by integrating feedback and coaching to improve their success and effectiveness. Feedback and coaching provides an objective perspective that can help a person become more self-aware, to understand their own internal dialogues and to begin to see the things that drive and motivate them. This process of being open to feedback and coaching and then undergoing honest introspection is something Larry refers as "self-observation without judgment."

- **Integrate them with higher maturity level people.** Consider the following scenario: Three young adults are together and a high-functioning adolescent, who is a peer, joins the conversation. Given the effects of peer pressure, the fourth person will adjust their behaviors upward and act more adult-like because of the prevailing number of adults. Whether that adolescent can integrate that new behavior or simply adapt and mimic in that moment is an important thing to consider in creating a business environment.

If you have a high-functioning adolescent culture and want to change, the best way is to add new adult talent to your team. With the right support, their influence will begin to change the team for the better. It is also noteworthy that as we create a more "adult-centric" business culture, some people will inevitably move on, or leave just to protect themselves. I think that any cultural process worth its investment will jettison 10%-20% of the staff over a two-year period.

I will admit I did not really start to consistently stretch into the adult phase until I was probably in my late 40s. Most of the time, I was a high-functioning adolescent who got away with murder for many, many years because I delivered great results. Being very competitive, I was looking for an edge to be better, faster, or more successful than anyone else. I always wanted the territory with the best set of customers, I wanted to monopolize the best resources, and I always worked the system to ensure they were always available for me. I rationalized my "all about me" behavior because I believed that selling was not a team sport, it was a "me" sport. Again, all this was tolerated and even encouraged because at the end of the day—or the 13 week cycle—I delivered the numbers. This is the tragedy of high-functioning adolescents. Business today, especially command-and-control cultures, rewards short-term results. Early on employees are trained to be fire fighters. Any adolescent behavior they may display is forgiven if the problems they are tasked with are solved. In this way, adolescents are rewarded and the cycle runs full loop. It does not take long before this behavior becomes intractable. Our colleagues in the workplace see those behaviors, see them rewarded, and begin to model them.

The answer here is not to eliminate all high-functioning adolescents and try to build an organization centered on maturity overnight. As with so many things, timing is the key. I recall a time I was replacing my Director of Operations, who I helped move onto another key role in the company. During the same time, Cisco was largely a command-and-control oriented company while my team and I were moving from command-and-control to a collaborative leadership style. It came down to a best and final candidate. His style was collaborative and he had a proven track record of delivering results in a company similar to Cisco. I decided to hire him.

To make a long story short, the lesson learned was that, in spite of our team moving to a collaborative leadership style, the rest of Cisco was still command-and-control. I underestimated the amount of time and people interface required for this person to be successful in Cisco's culture. In retrospect, he was Type B collaborative and needed to be Type A collaborative. I should have hired a high-functioning adolescent leader with great potential for adult-like behaviors. They could have been successful in Cisco's current mode of operations while being prepared for the next-gen leadership style of collaboration.

LEVELING UP

High-performing teams have high-performing relationships. You cannot have high-performing relationships without authentic communications. Conventional conversation theory cites two levels of exchange:

- **Level 1 conversations are rooted in exchanging data and facts.** In Level 1 conversations, we may discuss the weather, traffic, scores from last night's game. People are most comfortable with having Level 1 conversations. In fact, people generally break the ice with Level 1 comments, or small talk, when meeting someone new. It is safe ground that everyone can access. Level 1 conversations are polite and are accompanied with little to no risk and stress.

- **Level 2 conversations are rooted in sharing more intimate thoughts, ideas, and opinions.** In Level 2 conversations, we express our personal views on any range of subjects from music to politics to business decisions. The distinction here is that during an interaction with another person or in a group, we begin to have an internal dialogue that is deeper, more personal, more risky, and more intimate than the public conversation. In respectful conversations, we announce when we are entering Level 2 conversations with qualifiers like, "in my opinion" or "from my perspective." If we give feedback, we might ask permission to do so—"Can I give you some feedback?" For example, let us say you are in a meeting and one of your peers, Bob, is discussing a situation that you are familiar with. Bob is misrepresenting some of the data and is putting a spin on the story that makes you look bad. You might say, "I need to have a Level 2 conversation about this discussion. I am trying to listen and be supportive, but frankly, I am having a hard time, Bob, because I personally disagree with what you are saying and how you are representing what happened. I'd like to put my perspective into this conversation."

As an added dimension, Level 2 conversations are also more about feelings. In my Level 2 conversations, I share more about how I feel about situations, issues, or ideas.

My personal experience with Level 2 conversations is they are like the layers of an onion being peeled back until you get to the core of what matters.

Conversations become more authentic when they steer further away from the mundane and get closer to how people sincerely think and feel. High-performing teams regularly give each other permission to get beyond Level 1 conversations. Effective Level 2 conversations develop from the heart and are couched in respect. For instance, when giving feedback, which is all about expressing your opinion about someone's behavior or ideas, it is best to be nonjudgmental, objective, and caring—basically, you want to put yourself in the receiver's shoes.

Developing a culture of Level 2 discussions, giving people permission to speak freely and to be genuine will heighten your ability to have quality interactions, make informed decisions and deliver bigger, better, faster results. As leaders, your job is to use Level 2 communications to put issues on the table, to discuss them with absolute and caring honesty, and make sure they do not come off the table until they are resolved.

A great way to engender a culture of Level 2 communication and to enable of sense of connection is to use a personal check-in at the beginning of team meetings. I picked up this practice from Larry Liberty. At the beginning of my leadership team meetings, we began to use the first 15 minutes to have personal check-ins. In a personal check-in, team members take time to share a bit of personal information with the rest of the team. It allows everyone to revalidate themselves and each other as human beings with real lives and real difficulties before digging into deep business discussions.

The check-in presents an opportunity for everybody to share one small fact about himself or herself or one thing that is going on in their lives. By acknowledging the other side of people's lives, we begin to understand what it might be like to be them for a day, a week, and a minute. With that understanding and empathy comes trust. With a check-in, you give permission for a Level 2 dialogue. When a team gets into the practice of having authentic check-ins they take the time to care. When you care about somebody, when you have a relationship, you will be more honest with him or her. When you achieve that level of discourse, people get all views on the table, which makes for better-informed decisions. At the end of the day, it is about results and it is about the team moving forward. That cannot happen unless relationships come first.

A HORSE OF A DIFFERENT COLOR

When presenting to large groups, I like to ask how many people have had a mentor. Even though everyone instinctively knows they should have one, a show of hands usually reveals that less than 10% actually do. Mentoring can be an effective development tool if used correctly. Over the years, I have seen three different approaches to mentoring:

- The first is the **traditional mentor program** in which a senior leader takes time to work with a more junior staff member, passing on wisdom, advice, and tips that may help them through their career. Traditional mentor programs are reactive and the mentor provides guidance from the sidelines.

- The second is **reverse mentoring.** I learned this concept from my team running our Inclusion and Diversity program. Most see a mentor as a person with more experience working and sharing with a less experienced person. However, in this case, it is the less experienced (usually younger) employee mentoring a senior leader, sharing what a day in their life is like, what attitudes and beliefs they have about the company and then sharing what they value in their job. This may be uncomfortable at first, but the experience is win–win for everyone.

- The third type is not really mentoring at all but is what we call **sponsorship.** While a mentor is a trusted counselor, guide, tutor, or coach, mostly in a passive role, a sponsor is someone who is willing to put some real skin in the game and break down barriers in order to assist their mentee. Their skin in the game is their good name and reputation which they are staking on the mentee's potential as a high performer. In addition to being a mentor, a sponsor creates opportunities via the three E's—experience, education and exposure—and proactively assists their mentee in advancing their careers.

Implementing a formal mentorship program is an easy and quick way to develop your team. While a mentor program can be good for an employee and even the mentor, a sponsor is necessary for any employee who has a credible track record and wants to advance their career. The additional benefit to a sponsorship is because the sponsor does feel some heat, they will try extra hard to make sure their mentee receives the development they need to truly succeed.

It is up to you, not your manager or leader, to find that special mentor to become your sponsor.

LITMUS TEST

Larry Liberty often says, "Leadership is the ability to bring out the best in others and the best in you." Building on that mantra, I had three specific goals in mind in using Larry's maturity factor with my team.

First, I wanted to make our staff meetings more productive. Leadership meetings are a key indicator for how the rest of the organization functions. If the leadership team is bickering with each other and creating roadblocks to productivity, they are going to lead their teams with the same behaviors and their teams will model them. Leadership staff meetings are the time and place to make decisions, create strategy and context, and deal with larger issues that require the entire team to act rationally and wisely. Leadership meetings are where policy is set, culture is modeled, performance is tracked and rewarded, interventions determined and difficult decisions made about people, capital expenditures, operational expense and other resources.

Second, I wanted my team to self-govern. Command-and-control is easy, but in a collaborative model, I did not want to play the policeman with the team. Self-governance was an end-state goal and it took time and patience for us to get there. This goal was critical, as these leaders were the team of men and women who would lead our organization through transformation and into growth. The team, and hence the meetings, would be the collaborative core of the theatre and as such I needed to create a level of guidance and leadership that is seldom experienced in large corporate settings. The team had to be a great example of a high performance leadership team and thus become a role model for others on their respective teams as well as within the larger Cisco organization.

Third, I wanted to shift the makeup of our team to more adult behavior as opposed to high-functioning adolescent behavior. Leadership meetings are no place for adolescents, high functioning or otherwise. If team members were incapable of consistent adult behavior and wanted to stay with a command-and-control leadership style, I would invite them to do so with a different team. Some did. With adult behavior in the room, we carved out the handhold we needed to pull ourselves to higher levels of performance.

The litmus test I used along the way to measure our progress was a series of questions I posed to our team on a regular basis. As noted earlier, one of the key behaviors to being a great salesperson is asking great questions. The same applies to leadership. Over time, we worked to answer these questions through Level 2 discussions, "adult" behaviors, and learning to leave the adolescents in the schoolyard.

1. *How do you see yourself in your peer group within your organization? Superior? Inferior? Equal? All of the above? Why?*

2. *Do you behave as if you belong on one team with your peer group?*

3. *Are you willing to put the success of the team or organization above your personal success?*

4. *Do you work toward win-win results with your customers? Staff? Peers?*

5. *Do you take on the tough topics when they need to be taken on?*

6. *Do you know what factors within you may be inhibiting your own success?*

7. *Do you have confidence in yourself as a leader?*

8. *Do you instill trust in your customers? Staff? Peers?*

9. *Do you have credibility with your customers? Staff? Peers?*

10. *Do you have the desire to develop and improve your capabilities as a leader?*

Initially, my team struggled with these questions and wanted to avoid answering them. Avoidance is a dangerous tool that high-functioning adolescents leverage. They feel that if they just wait long enough the pressure for business results will make it go away. Denial, by the way, is another survival tool of adolescents. As a leader, this is another blink test you will have to face.

In the end, my team and I became proficient in responding to the questions in real and relevant ways, with actions and behaviors as opposed to rhetoric and excuses. I have heard it said that high-performing teams make the extraordinary look ordinary. Working with Larry Liberty helped us to do just that. Along the way, we also developed some simple but powerful tools of the trade to help us in some very pragmatic ways. These tools will be the subject of Chapter Eleven.

INSTANT REPLAY

One of the most impactful tools you can use in developing staff is focusing on the maturity level of your employees . . . as well as yourself. Larry Liberty suggests that just as people develop physiologically from infancy to adolescence to adulthood, so people develop psychologically as well. The unique dynamics of a workplace highlight a person's developmental stage especially well. A typical workplace is populated mostly with high-functioning adolescents and young adults. Sprinkled amongst the organization may also be the rare wise adults. While all of these levels of maturity can function in a workplace, the level of contention as well as calm they may generate varies. The simple rule is the higher level of maturity, the more stability. Depending on the stage of an organization—and again, what is needed—a leader should strive to level up the maturity level from adolescence to adulthood.

Maturity is a key factor in having high-performing relationships. One of the markers of high-performing relationships is Level 2 conversations. While Level 1 conversations are rooted in exchanging data and facts, Level 2 conversations are rooted in sharing more intimate thoughts, ideas, and opinions. When people become versed in having Level 2 conversations and, more importantly, when they become comfortable with allowing them, everything from decision making to the ability to prioritize improves.

Ways to help staff move through the maturity levels include coaching, opportunities for self-insight, immersion with people of higher maturity levels and different forms of mentoring such as traditional mentoring, reverse mentoring, and sponsorship.

The litmus test I used, both with myself and with my team to coax us into higher levels of maturity, was a series of questions that we posed to ourselves on a regular basis. The key was to answer them without blinking, to be brutally honest with each other and ourselves. It took some time before we could answer most of the questions to our satisfaction. The idea is not to answer them "correctly," but rather to have the discussion, talk about what matters and how we as a leadership team can improve over time.

CHAPTER TEN

NEVER WASTE A GOOD CRISIS

In this chapter, I will describe a systematic approach to **change** which will then lead to a systematic approach to **transformation.** Before transformation can commence, an organization needs to undergo fundamental changes in the way it operates. Organizational change involves tangible adjustments to how the organization operates from a process and people perspective. Organizational transformation involves intangible adjustments to how an organization functions from a leadership and cultural perspective. A complete transformation approach includes everything from vision to execution to governance to culture to leadership, and all the bits in between. If it sounds challenging, it is.

To impose order on the chaos, to systematize change that sets the foundation for transformation, you first need sufficient motivation.

My dad once told me, "Kid, never waste a good crisis." When things fall apart, the need for order becomes paramount. Although no one wants to deal with a crisis, you should never let one go to waste. A crisis presents the perfect time for dramatic improvements that may have been too large to implement during peace time. The simple fact is that while people are difficult to motivate when things are going well, a crisis gets their attention and drums out complacency. A crisis sends a clear message to everyone about a shared and urgent problem. A crisis is a perfect platform for foundational change—and if you are going to implement that kind of change, you should make sure the results truly make the organization more competitively fit.

After the crisis is over, everyone expects to get back to business as usual. Do not be led down that path, as some things, important things, will never be the same again.

Over my last 11 years at Cisco, we faced a number of challenges, both internal and external. One of the major challenges we took on was the myriad of economic woes that was set off by the dotcom implosion. The bursting of the dotcom bubble was followed by the market slow down, and then a sub-prime financial services meltdown. The burning platform was obvious to everyone. When Cisco found the need to hit the reset button, I borrowed space on that burning platform to galvanize my organization for additional changes and improvements. Although my services sales organization was not in a crisis, I knew that productivity and sales could be better. I was not going to let a crisis go to waste.

In Cisco, we had a 10/10 rule. The 10/10 rule dictates that you have to increase your productivity by 10% each year to keep your operational expense (OPEX) flat. Quite simply, if you wanted more OPEX, your productivity needed to be stretched further than 10%. If your forecast was flat to the previous year, then you took a 10% cut in OPEX, which typically meant taking people out of the business. What started as a push to finish 10% better than your target became a kind of productivity tax. If you wanted to grow, well, you needed to stretch your targets (and results) further. Each year in our organization we would build a set of scenarios—a flat scenario, taking out 10%; a productivity tax scenario, growing 10%; and a stretch scenario, growing 20%. For each scenario, we plotted out the conditions and assumptions that predicated success. Essentially we had to decide on the "what" and the growth percent associated with it. My goal for the services sales organization was the stretch scenario plus another 10% to invest in innovation. I wanted to transform the business by 30+% growth. The opportunity for me, therefore, was born of four factors:

1. We needed substantial business transformation to cover the productivity tax, growth, plus innovation investment. There was no way we could rest on our laurels and let the market get the best of us.

2. We needed to leverage the power of inclusion and diversity to change the organizational culture, a culture marked by "dive and catch" players, activity focused management and passive/aggressive leaders. The type of change we needed would require a groundswell of management support and leadership effort. A single person could not accomplish what needed to be done.

3. We would not be given a reprieve from delivering results during transformation. Quite simply, Cisco was not going to give us a break for two to three years. In the end, we proved that transformation could be managed simultaneously with running and growing a business as we delivered $36-billion of revenue and $20-billion of contribution margin to Cisco over 11 years.

These three factors paled in comparison to the fourth factor. Over time, I came to recognize the biggest issue facing my team was a manager vs. leader gap.

4. I had a team of managers who were keen on the "how" and the "who," but I needed them to be leaders to solve the "what" and the "why." To do so I had to break these managers of trying to build the future based on the past, of reaching into the same bag of tricks that yielded the same results that were inadequate to the task ahead of us. I knew we could not resolve items 1 – 3 without resolving this gap.

As I stepped back and considered how we were going to hit progressively growing stretch targets quarter on quarter, year on year, I knew I had to help my team bridge the leadership gap. I took it as a personal challenge, a leadership challenge in both senses of the word—a difficulty that has to be overcome, and a provocation, a call to step up and make a difference. The equation to be solved was not comprised of performance targets; it was comprised of embedding sustainable leadership behaviors. This was not a crisis that could be solved by a stirring five-minute speech in the locker room. The problem was too big and too systemic. It was going to take a vision, strategy, a plan, focused execution, lots of leadership fortitude, and the right culture. It was going to take a systematic approach.

COLLABORATIVE TRANSFORMATION APPROACH

Collaborative transformation is a way of transforming a company culture from primarily command-and-control (C&C) into a culture where leaders can solidly work from a teamwork-and-collaboration (T&C) base and leverage C&C when strategically necessary, as discussed in Chapter Seven.

Over the last 20 years of my successes and failures, a structured approach has emerged, which I have dubbed the Collaborative Transformation Approach (CTA). CTA comprises a set of processes, tools, and practices for diverse organizations to come together and intuitively create a collaborative environment. The success or failure of this environment depends on how effectively you can enable adaptive systems.

"An adaptive system is a set of interacting or interdependent entities, real or abstract, forming an integrated whole that together are able to respond to environmental changes or changes in the interacting parts."[8] Teamwork-and-collaboration is one form of an adaptive system, so lets explore how to leverage it further.

So what exactly are we talking about? In the business world, adaptive systems...

- Are resilient to changes in leadership
- Make data-driven decisions and have realistic goals
- Respond to problems with innovative solutions
- Naturally align cultural values
- Generate their own sustaining energy
- Are self-correcting
- Make the right decisions without seeking approval from above

---

[8] Juan Ange Garcia-Pardo Gimenez de los Galanes. "Social Based Adaption in Multi-agent Systems." Master's Thesis. November 2010. http://riunet.upv.es/bitstream/handle/10251/13702/Thesis_master.pdf?sequence=1

Adaptive systems range from simple to complex. Complex adaptive systems are required when you have very large companies, where organizations are multidimensional and free flowing. Typically, the lines of organizational responsibility are blurred and exist within multiple organizations.

> *"Any fool can make things more complex, it takes courage to go in the other direction."*
>
> —ALBERT EINSTEIN

Consider a large sales organization like Cisco. The sales organization may break down into products and services, with subgroups aligned by geographical theatres, and sub-sub-groups aligned by segment (enterprise, commercial, service provider, and public) or vertical customer business types. When these organizations need to work together, to prevent them from going into chaos, they need overlapping cultural values (e.g., "doing the right thing for the customer" or "the customer is always right") that provide common understanding. With hundreds or thousands of people, it becomes increasingly difficult to communicate, integrate, and align these values. This is where C&C, a non-adaptive system, breaks down. As more C&C managers are added to the mix, often with competing value-systems, more conflicts arise and passive aggressive behavior becomes the norm. These conflicts permeate the organization, and it becomes harder and harder to sustain a common (corporate) culture.

There simply are not enough hours in the day for C&C managers to effectively manage this level chaos and complexity. In contrast, an adaptive system, like teamwork-and-collaboration, generates its own energy. An adaptive system grows on its own. People come together when given a solvable problem, they know they will get approval and they know they have a fair chance of success. Decision-making is forced to the lowest point possible, to the person most qualified to make the decision because they have the necessary data and right experience. The decision is usually the "right" decision for the company, as well as the individual and the organization.

CTA enables all of these benefits by taking the sometimes unwieldy aspects of running an enterprise business and bringing them into balance in a way that enables adaptive systems to thrive. As illustrated, below CTA covers four areas: Leadership, Governance, Vision/Strategy/Execution (VSE), and Culture.

All these areas work in collaboration with each other. VSE can't exist without leadership guidance; leadership is purposeless without governance; governance is empty without culture; culture is directionless without VSE. As we have discussed leadership in some detail on its own, let's explore three of these areas in more detail and see how leadership intertwines through them.

GOVERNANCE: ALPHABET SOUP

Many people view governance as a set of protocols and rules by which a business is policed. Most people describe governance through alphabet soup acronyms like RACI, CAIRO, RAPID, and other responsibility matrices.[9] Have no doubt these models are important, as they help deliver governance via documented processes and agreements. The value of responsibility matrices is that they create a reference point, a document that everyone can see, agree upon, and hold each other accountable to. For me, however, governance is more than a set of responsibilities and ownership delineation. It is the syntax between the practices and processes that set boundaries (via policies) and provide structure for strategic execution. True governance is the act of order imposed upon chaos. For instance, portfolio and project management are underpinned by the governance acts of prioritization and decision-making. Solid governance enables an organization to get ahead of where they need to be, whether it is staying flat in a declining market or funding self-growth through innovation investment. Governance ensures that the right people for the right reasons are making the right decisions at the right time.

Also within the scope of governance are the systems, tools, processes, and training needed to usher in change and transformation. Change management under the umbrella of governance is critically important as governance enables an organization to move forward. Change management is about giving people the tools they need to make effective change happen in a productive way. Change management helps to differentiate the core from the context and to drive out inefficiencies and redundancies.

Key to change management are portfolio and project management disciplines. Each is a separate discipline but each one supports the other. For example, project management is about execution. Change management places the boundaries around the execution. Portfolio management is about prioritizing change. Each has its own tracking tool.

---

[9] Common responsibility and decision making matrices include RACI (responsible, accountable, consulted, informed), CAIRO (consulted, accountable, informed, responsible, out of the loop), RAPID (recommend, agree, perform, input, decide).

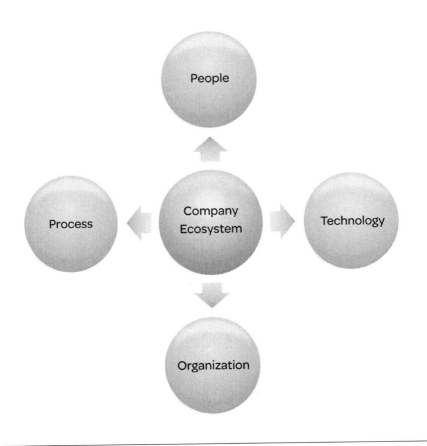

A company is like an ecosystem made up of people, process, technology, and organization (PPTO). When any aspect of the PPTO ecosystem is changed, it affects the rest of the ecosystem. When one of the four changes, leaders should anticipate and plan for the effects on the other three.

VSE: THE NEXUS OF SUCCESS

The nexus of a successful organization is the triad of vision, strategy and execution. **Vision** sets a compelling direction for the business and establishes what success looks like. It is the rallying cry for "why" the organization exists and inspires an organization about the future. As I described earlier, vision is the team's shared goals, what they have agreed to accomplish together as an organization. Set by the leadership of the organization, vision is agreed to and supported by the organization itself, from leaders to managers to individual contributors. The key drivers here are communication and alignment.

For a vision to take hold it first has to be communicated throughout the organization, from top to bottom, as well outside the organization to external stakeholders. As you may imagine, how vision is communicated is tightly related to culture. Next, there must be alignment around that vision from the leaders who communicate it to the organization that enables it.

Strategy, as we previously discussed, is the what and the why. Leadership owns strategy and through it accounts for the external and internal drivers that shape market dynamics. One of the most straightforward definitions of strategy I have read is from Ed Barrows: "A business strategy specifies the way a firm competes in an industry."[10] That "way" is informed by an industry-based analysis of the competitive landscape, the legal and regulatory environment, industry product and service innovation, and other dynamics. If vision describes what success looks like, strategy provides focus and indicates how realistic and how rewarding reaching that vision may actually be.

As with vision, there has to be leadership alignment and true communication for strategy to be successful. If alignment to the vision does not exist, conflicting strategies tied to differing perceptions of the vision will collide. While this is sometimes the result of miscommunication, it is more often the result of passive/aggressive management styles.

Execution defines the "how" and the "who" of delivering the strategy that will realize the vision. This is done via detailed work breakdown structures and project plans. Execution is generally owned by management. As with vision and strategy, alignment is essential. Execution without line of sight to vision and strategy is misdirected effort and often results in business disruption and underperformance. Key enablers of successful execution are a decision making process, in conjunction with authorized and clearly communicated

---

[10] http://www.edbarrows.com/Resources/briefs/BusinessStrategyDefined.pdf

accountabilities. Measurement should be a part of execution. Execution has to be measured against front-end loaded objectives.

One reason why people are not successful in execution is that they always plan for success. You need to have a plan for failure as well.

CULTURE: IT NEVER TAKES A DAY OFF

Culture is the single most difficult thing for a large business to get right because it is solely dependent on the people factor—that is, culture requires people to make it happen and people are capricious by nature. Culture is both an input and an output of leadership, governance, and VSE. Culture is a virtuous cycle of an organization's attitudes, beliefs, and values which manifests itself in behaviors, ethics and, yes, performance. While a healthy culture on its own cannot guarantee healthy commercial results—the other components of a CTA are required—an ailing culture will **always** yield suboptimal results.

Culture is about shared values, but what happens when you have a number of subcultures with opposing values? The answer is the culture begins to breakdown. Due care must be taken to nurture and grow a healthy culture. The problem is how do you begin shaping something so intangible?

First, culture must start with a small population that is amenable to alignment around a single, simple vision. Then, decide who can powerfully carry forward that vision as evangelists who will, in turn, inspire true believers. That special population is leaders. Leaders must take care to build culture into the strategy, processes and protocol of an organization—namely, through governance and Vision, Strategy & Execution (VSE)—and they must also take care to build it into the fabric of an organization through relationships. For instance, teamwork-and-collaboration can be built into a governance model, but without underscoring that intent with relationships and incentives, it is likely to fall flat.

In addition, culture needs the rich input of diverse perspectives. Diversity is not about race, religion, color or the symbols of diversity, it is about differences. I have always found it valuable to bring into an organization people who have different experiences and backgrounds. Nothing is more dangerous than homogeneous thinking.

Bringing in diversity is one thing; actually doing something with it is another. Leaders need to listen to those perspectives and act upon them. It strikes me that 90% of what ails an organization could be solved if the organization only knew what it knows. By this, I mean people in an organization have insights into problems and solutions that leadership will pay a consultancy firm a fortune to discover when all they need to do is to listen to their own people.

> *"Human capital is by far the most important asset any company has. Preserving employees' autonomy and infusing healthy competition is the best way to get the most out of employees."*
>
> —MAHESH RAO, Founder & CEO of Quest 2 Excel, Inc. (Q2E)

 **INSTANT REPLAY**

To really drive business transformation an organization needs to change how it does its work. Transformation does not just happen—at least not effective and sustainable transformation. As noted many times, people do not like to change; therefore, transformation must have a compelling reason and a focused purpose. An important lesson I learned early in my career was to never waste a good crisis. Never waste the opportunity a crisis affords to galvanize an organization around a common goal and never waste your efforts trying to implement change through ineffective means. The foundation of transformation is change management. Many businesses approach change through organizational design or by tweaking their business model. The most effective means to exercise change is a method I call the Collaborative Transformation Approach, or CTA. A Collaborative Transformation Approach involves a systemic and holistic approach encompassing leadership, governance, VSE (vision, strategy, and execution) and culture.

- **Leadership** influences all areas. None of the aspects of CTA can function effectively without strong leadership. It establishes the vision, sets the strategy, authorizes execution, monitors governance and influences culture.

- **Governance** guides and sets boundaries for vision, strategy and execution and has a tremendous impact of culture. It also influences leadership by establishing the rules of engagement by defining decision making rights and mapping out roles and responsibilities.

- **Vision, Strategy and Execution** are collectively a business's raison d'etre, its plan for success as well as the means to make it all happen.

- **Culture** is at the core of CTA. Culture is both an input and an output of all the above. Its breadth and depth can be increased through diversity and its impact on an organization can be better ensured through relationship building and listening.

A collaborative approach to transformation can yield strong results and minimize distractions to your business. The real benefit may be that it can also provide better work life integration and build a culture that enables trust in the people working for you to make the "right" decisions.

CHAPTER ELEVEN

LIONS AND TIGERS AND BEARS

In the early 2000s, I saw an opportunity to transform the Cisco service sales business that I led. To do this I had to do more than simply meet Cisco's requirement for growth, I had to outpace Cisco's 10% productivity tax to self-fund enough investment to enable the transformation. As a sales and services organization, we needed our own plan or we ran the risk of becoming part of someone else's plan.

As I looked across my organization, I saw talented people leveraging massive amounts of human capital trying to do the right thing. I also saw many people pulling very hard in different directions causing inefficiencies, ineffectiveness, and a souring culture. It was clear to me that in order to obtain the growth we needed for our future, we had to clean up our act and get serious about superior performance driving for superior results. I knew we could not get there with a staff full of managers focused on "the who and the how" with no one attending to "the what and the why."

At an off-site strategy meeting I asked my segment leaders (enterprise, commercial, public sector, service provider, and channel) to present their growth plans for the next three years. This in itself was interesting as most of Cisco planned quarterly against an annual target. True to form, each one came prepared with a specific set of goals and results based on their own segment needs for a single year. I remember watching presentation after presentation, realizing there was no way we could reach our growth objectives in our current state because everybody wanted to optimize their own segment without considering the overall effect. It was a classic case in which optimizing the parts failed to optimize the whole. It was at that time that I began to take the actions that would, upon reflection, make up the constituent parts of a collaborative transformation approach.

RUN, GROW, TRANSFORM

From that off-site strategy meeting emerged two simple goals for the services sales business: one, improve the effectiveness of the organization; two, improve the efficiency of the organization. To do this, we needed to examine the fundamental core and context of our business.

Core, as it is has traditionally been defined, applies to processes that differentiate your offers to create competitive advantage leading to customer preference. *Context* refers to all other processes. The overwhelming bulk of all work is context, not core. The goal for managing context is productivity, freeing up resources to repurpose for core. We utilized this core vs. context framework to examine all of our selling activities (see Figure 1 on Page 209).

We embedded our goals of effectiveness and efficiency in a run/grow/ transform strategy to deliver more value to our customers and partners so that we could self-fund transformation. The strategy was simply to move the business through three phases:

- In **run,** we would ensure we met our performance targets every 13 weeks. Running the business in a profitable way was non-negotiable. It was our license to operate.

- **Grow** the business meant just that. We would grow margin and volume, expanding the depth and breadth of our customer base.

- **Transform** required that the work done in run and grow were sustainable for the long-term. Transform required change.

A run/grow/transform strategy works in several ways. The sweet spot is to have all your offerings and go-to-market fully optimized for efficiency and effectiveness during the "run" portion of the lifecycle. It all starts at the project level and proposing a new service to meet a customer's need. If it successfully meets the customer's need and if it is scalable, profitable, and repeatable, it becomes part of a solution set of offerings to deliver specific business outcomes. The final steps include gaining critical market mass, then scaling through a multi-channel route to market. In our case, the challenge was that most of the OPEX funding for the run stage was five to ten times lower than what was going to be required to build the grow and transform stages.

To help us in our endeavor, we collaborated with Geoffrey Moore and two principals of The Chasm Group, Lo-Ping Yeh and Todd Hewlin. Together we embarked on a productivity workout process that helped us to hone in on our objectives—improve the effectiveness and efficiency—with laser-like sharpness.

We took the classic workshop approach with a cross-functional team across each segment to identify and analyze each step in service sales engagement. Because the team was built from representatives (approx. 35) the businesses respected, the team had a tremendous amount of credibility—they also had a tremendous responsibility to report real actionable findings back to their respective segment. Using the frame of core vs. context, the team examined over 300 individual tasks and activities.

Our work on **improving effectiveness** focused on aligning the right skill sets to the right activities to increase revenues, decrease costs, and protect margins with an end goal of funding long-term transformation. During the workshops, we found we had talented, experienced people all doing the same activities. This was actually two issues wrapped in one. First was the matter of replicating the same activities repeatedly, especially in a sales cycle. Second was the matter of mismatching people's skill sets and incentive plans for the work they were doing. In some cases the resources were under-qualified for what they were assigned. In other instances they were over-compensated for their assigned responsibilities.

Our work on **improving efficiency** concentrated on eliminating duplication, process gaps, and rework. The primary problem here was that every segment felt their way of doing things uniquely suited their needs. What emerged were scores of differing processes to deliver against the same needs albeit in different locations.

Another piece of the puzzle was that our systems were from the late 90s and built to run a $500-million services business not a $5-billion services business. Although they were being reengineered, they could only do so much at the time. We were filling the gaps with a lot of manual labor. We were also reworking mountains of data. Our business for the US and Canada theatre ran on approximately 1.7 million transactions annually. In the efficiency arena, we wanted to minimize expenditure of time, effort and dollars.

The specific areas we started to probe were new service sales and low-dollar contracts. We discovered issues that had been sapping efficiency and effectiveness for years. Everyone knew they were out there, but until we conducted a careful analysis no one realized just how threatening these culprits were—or on the other side, how big of an opportunity they represented. For example, we found that 24% of the sales tasks and activities were focused on non-mission critical context. We will discuss this in more detail later, but 24% of our time spent on these activities was not a good use of our resources (see Figure 2 on Page 209). The issues were the lions, tigers, and bears stalking us through a dark forest, but they would soon become the prey (opportunities) and we became the hunters as we decided to face them in a systematic, uniform way.

We were to discover that to really drive business transformation we had to change how we as an organization did our work. Many businesses approach change through organizational design or by tweaking their business model.

Real transformation comes through a methodical, fact-based approach encapsulated with strong leadership and governance. Success comes when the culture shifts and the organization embraces the change with their heads, hearts and hands.

THREE GOLDEN EGGS

The analysis of new service sales, low-dollar contracts and the core versus context of sales activities revealed three golden eggs of opportunities. Nested with those opportunities was the means to substantially narrow the gap on our three-year growth goals.

Core and Context Framework

Core: An activity that end-customers and partners value sufficiently such that executing the activity twice as well would drive significantly higher revenue, margins, or both			Context: All other processes
		Core	Context
Mission Critical: An activity that if a company were to fail to execute the activity in a timely manner to parity there would be a substantial risk to the business	Mission Critical	Differentiation	Largest $$$$
Non-Mission Critical: All other processes	Non-Mission Critical	Emerging Differentiation	Opportunistic/ Waste

Figure 1

Core/Context Service Sales Analysis

		Process creates differentiation that wins customers	All other processes	
		Core	Context	
Process shortfall creates serious and immediate risk	Mission Critical	8%	67%	
All other processes	Non-Mission Critical	1%	24%	Validation of poor data and rework

Figure 2

We determined that "new and renewal services" was an activity common across all our segments and therefore rife with opportunities for standardizing processes and driving out redundancies. As suspected, we found every segment approached new services and renewals in their own way, unnecessarily duplicating effort and reworking data that other segments were also doing. For example, we asked each segment (a total of six) to bring an example of a "renewal quote" they provided to the customer. While each one had some common elements, they were all largely different. Now imagine that with 1.7 million transactions!

When the team focused on the "what," we also saw the chance to level set effective processes and methodologies. Instead of having pockets of excellence in various segments, we would shoot for consistent excellence in all segments. This became the first golden opportunity: To drive out inefficiencies, instill effectiveness and then standardize the improved practices across the theatre.

The second golden opportunity presented itself as we studied low-dollar contracts (LDCs). We discovered we could take advantage of "long tail" economics. In long tail economics, more of the sample lies in lengthy tail of the distribution than in the rest of the distribution. For us, although low-dollar contracts represented small value capture opportunity on a one-by-one basis, the value capture opportunity grew exponentially when we multiplied that value times the number of LDCs. What at first looked like a mildly interesting chance to land a few small gains become a tremendous opportunity for serious returns. For example, the overall services business was approximately 1.7 million transactions. However, 1.5 of the 1.7 million transactions were under $25-thousand, and that was the sweet spot for efficiency and effectiveness!

We discovered that the sales cycle required for the "low dollar contracts" was not much different from a renewal for over $250-thousand, as the same steps tools and processes were required to close the transaction. Due to this, the current organization focused their energy on the higher value renewals that provided a larger return on the time invested. This meant that a large number of accounts were not engaged or were engaged late in the sales cycle, usually after the contract had already expired, creating a lag in cash flow. This provided a large opportunity to improve cash flow, on-time renewals, customer satisfaction, and partner loyalty.

The third golden opportunity, which ended up as the primary solution to golden opportunity number two, started out as a way of looking at our sales activities end to end, which included selling and non-selling activities like contract management and administration. The perspective quickly resulted in a series of optimization efforts. Here our designation of core and context really came into play. Core, as noted earlier, was made up of activities that differentiated our business in the eye of our customers and partners. The context was everything else. The key in defining the core was not to consider what differentiated us from "our" viewpoint, but rather what differentiated us from the "customers and partners" viewpoint. In terms of the art and science, we had to put ourselves on the art side of the mirror.

The litmus test for identifying core activities versus context became: "Would the customer pay more or give us more business based on the activities?"

As we put our activities to the test, we realized that while we had 300 distinct tasks and activities, only 14 of those activities were unique to any particular segment. This was a big ah-ha moment because we focused on what people did vs. how and who did them. The next big ah-ha came when we uncovered that a full 24% of our people's time was spent on non-critical mission context activities which provided no value to our customers. If those activities were to disappear, the customers would never notice . . . and still we spent 24% of our time doing them! We were doing these tasks for no one except ourselves, and the truth was we did not need them either. It is alarming how much work is generated on activities that no one really needs. The amazing part is that we typically know that no one needs them but we continue to do them anyway.

As part of scrutinizing the core and context, we also sought to better understand risk. One lens we used was mission critical versus non-mission critical. Mission critical indicated that if there were a shortfall, serious and immediate risk would incur. Mission critical was the performance standard which the market expected from particular activities. Non-mission critical would be all other processes.

Similar to the broader core and context analysis, we wanted to determine how we were allocating our time and resources. The point was we needed to focus on core, mission critical activities, and not waste resources on context, non-mission critical efforts. Two actions that came out of the analysis were:

- Define specific roles to focus on core and mission critical activities. This addressed the problem of role clarity in the selling process that led to duplication of activities.

- Standardize and optimize processes to give time back to sales. This addressed non-value add activities that were consuming people's time and determined ways to eliminate, simplify or standardize the activities so staff could instead focus on mission critical and core activities.

The results seem incredibly simple but the analysis was a real revelation. They created a sense of urgency as well as a sense of confidence as the plank to safer ground became obvious to everyone. Efficiency and effectiveness were no longer platitudes splashed on a PowerPoint slide, but were real opportunities right there at our fingertips—sometimes literally. We knew where we wanted to go and we now had the means to get there. All we needed was to get people to come along with us. We had to enlist the heads, hearts and hands of the organization, including leaders, managers and individual contributors alike.

HEADS, HEARTS AND HANDS

As noted earlier, approximately 70% percent of people will reject an idea outright even if the idea is the absolute correct thing to go do. It's part of the pain theory of change management—if the pain of making a change is greater than the pain you have today, you will not make the change. It sounds ludicrous but it happens every day. Leaders, managers and organizations would rather do 80-100 hours of manual work per week than invest the OPEX and time to create a system to automate it. True to form, when we introduced our efficiency and effectiveness plans, the Cisco Services sales organization resisted.

To create buy-in, we first addressed the minds of the organization's thought leaders and then cascaded through the rest of the organization. We conducted workshops with representatives across all of the major key stakeholder groups inside our team. During the workshops we were able to get people to focus on the "what" of our processes as opposed to the "how and who." This helped people to see the commonality of processes and to divorce themselves from the notion that what they did was unique. By showing fact-based information that 95% of the activities were identical across all the segments, we provided an objective view that helped to open awareness and understanding, a key step to successful change management. People's belief in their distinctiveness from other segments and regions is what drove so many variant processes. In disengaging people from the discrete everyday processes that felt right because they were so ingrained as mental models, we were able to examine the processes holistically.

We discovered that *"status updates,"* which detailed where an order was in the booking process—a surprisingly mundane but time consuming activity—was duplicated across the entire sales process from vice presidents all the way down to individual services sellers. When we demonstrated this to people, we were able to move from engaging the minds of the organization to engaging their hearts. As it turns out, people are not as passionate about completing mundane tasks such as status updates, as they are about working on activities that add value to customers and partners as well as growth to business.

In Cisco's case the "status updates" become a hot button because of linearity and weekly commitments. Every 13 weeks sales numbers had to be hit in a cumulative climb to achieve the annual plan. Similarly, to ensure the 13-week targets were hit, weekly commitments were made that would build to the targets. Essentially, weekly commitments became part of the critical path to delivering the annual plan. As part of the critical path, everyone wanted on-demand visibility into the commitment process. The problem was that since Cisco's systems could not track the "weekly commit" at the frequency and accuracy people demanded, they began to gap fill with manual tracking. It did not take long before people were overwhelmed just by the forecast/commit process.

The key was stepping back and separating the "what" from the "how" and the "who." Although it sounds simple, it was a huge mental shift. Prior to the workshops, the approach was to allow each segment to run somewhat independently, which invariably became a hairball because of the perceived variations across the segments. By the time we had completed the last workshop we shared a common taxonomy to start constructing plans to standardize and optimize the sales process. With the heads and the hearts engaged, we could now enlist the hands.

From that point, we looked where process optimization opportunities lay and began to apply productivity levers we categorized as centralized, standardized, modularized and optimized. We prioritized key activity improvements, process optimization, and then identified interdependencies with other teams so we would not duplicate work that was already underway. This was an important alignment effort. Then we determined the skills sets needed for each activity to define distinct roles. In this way, we addressed the lack of role clarity.

Never confuse a change in coverage model or realignment of resources as transformation. Everyone, especially in sales, tries to execute a new offensive strategy assuming their team has the skills, abilities and experience to make it a success. It usually takes a systemic, holistic solution to fix a systemic, holistic problem.

As we moved through the process from design to implementation, we used the classic five leadership actions to maintain momentum:

1. We provided **strong executive sponsorship** around vision and alignment.

2. We leveraged **teamwork-and-collaboration** with a cross-segment team of managers, analysts and front-line subject matter experts and others key stakeholders to design the new end-to-end process.

3. We **educated and trained** people on our means and goals (what is in this for you if you do well and what are the consequences if you do poorly).

4. We took the time to **celebrate** successes and communicated rewards and recognition.

5. We **measured** progress against targets as part of our management metrics.

These actions only make up part of the story. In the background, we also created a culture of high-performing teams based upon an atmosphere of trust, personal-based relationships, and transparency and authenticity. The amazing thing was that the positive business results that started to roll in reinforced the positive culture of trust and accountability; the positive culture, in turn, further drove the positive results. As we delivered against plan every 13 weeks, we picked up momentum. True to our first order of business—run—the drive to meet performance targets never went away. By using the components of the collaborative transformation approach (as discussed in Chapter Ten), we were able to generate momentum that with the support of a strong culture soon created its own momentum.

NAVIGATING THE LABYRINTH

We started the Cisco Services sales growth initiative in the Fall of 2006 with an estimated end date of 2010. It was a multi-year initiative and we faced many, many obstacles along the way—some foreseen, others unforeseen. The impulse of people undergoing change is to revert to former practices; that is, to do things the "old way." The role of the leader is to pass the blink test, to hold true to the cause and make course corrections along the way. If you blink, the organization will rush back to the other side of the mirror rather than face change. Leading through this type of change requires more than science, it takes the 10,000 hours of experience, self-awareness and a commitment to vision.

Avoid trying to boil the ocean—try focusing on no more than three areas that will have the maximum amount of impact as opposed to trying to cure every ill. To avoid overwhelming an organization and to sharpen focus, leaders must hone in on the "what" and the "why" which will, in turn, surface the right tactical solutions.

In Greek mythology the labyrinth was a complex maze that held captive a ferocious Minotaur who himself was an obstacle for those who dared enter the structure. At times during the Cisco Services sales transformation I felt we were making our way through own labyrinth, working through obstacles and false turns to eventually take on our nemesis. We certainly made our fair share of mistakes along the way or, to be politically correct, we became aware of several opportunities to improve.

- The first leadership opportunity was to rectify a tendency to develop blind spots toward favored employees. For whatever reasons, leaders and managers alike can become overly loyal to some employees who no longer deliver value at the correct level. This saps morale and productivity from an organization.

- The second was to correct a propensity for leaders and managers to overestimate the organization's capacity. Capacity relates to the amount of work an organization can take on at any given time. Leaders are at times like college professors who think their students have no other course work except for theirs. There is always a large body of work that is invisible to leaders but which consumes hours and hours of an employee's daily work. Leaders do not always understand how much time and effort it takes to get certain things done, and they inadvertently overload teams and organizations.

- The third was related to the second in that it affects capacity. We had the opportunity to overcome the habit of leaders and managers to shy away from saying "no." In an effort to strengthen internal and external relationships they say "yes" to projects, initiatives and additional work that can add significant burden to an organization, strip away flexibility and cause distractions. If that was not bad enough, work–life integration also goes out of balance.

- The fourth was unlearning the tendency to underestimate duration and costs. Project managers often times fail to build in additional time and resources needed to compensate for the realities of multiple priorities, both business and personal employee issues. Perhaps they are initially built in and then stripped out later to meet cost challenges. Either way, leaders are often overly optimistic in their estimation of duration and cost. Sadly, most everyone knows to under-commit and over-deliver, but the opposite normally occurs.

In addition to leadership opportunities, I also saw broader organizational opportunities.

- One was that many of our managers were still in the process of shifting from focusing on the "how" and the "who" to focusing on the "what" and the "why." Leadership transformation takes time and every person will adjust to different timelines based on their experience, competencies and willingness to change. Do not give up on transformation if you do not see immediate results. It takes at least two years for this level of change to happen. Know this and plan for it by providing appropriate support mechanisms.

- Another issue was the constant pressure of linearity. The drive to perform weekly can sometimes cause disabling behaviors that detract from delivering the larger transformation goals. This can happen in senior leaders just as easily as more junior staff—and with more destructive impact. A leader who demands a daily, or in week 13, hourly status updates with unexpected data requests can cost an organization hundreds of unanticipated labor hours and cause undue loss of productivity.

- The final organizational issue was underestimating behavioral and cultural inertia. It does not happen just because someone wrote it on a PowerPoint. The Cisco service sales transformation took nearly four years not because that was the total duration of the estimated activities and tasks lined up end to end, but because transformation isn't just a matter of science, it's a matter of art and art can get messy.

Addressing these complexities, plus the pragmatic everyday issues of running a business was no easy task, but in the end what started as an efficiency and effectiveness program to self-fund growth became a full-on business transformation. The result was our expense to bookings percentage decreased dramatically every year while at the same time our bookings increased. As time was freed up from non-mission critical context activities, it was reallocated to core value-add activities such as advanced services. As we grew advanced services, our customer satisfaction and customer loyalty indexes grew. From the art side of the mirror, nothing is better than growing customer loyalty as well as the services business as that begins a virtuous cycle of growth. In the next chapter we will discuss the glue that makes change stick—relationships.

 **INSTANT REPLAY**

When leaders talk about change management, they show the traditional graphic of a platform being overwhelmed by fire. Leading from the burning platform to a safe platform is a stable, secure plank. The burning platform for the Cisco

Services sales organization was the tumultuous effects of the dotcom implosion plus challenging market dynamics and a souring economy. The secure bridge that promised escape from ruin and delivery to growth was a system to drive efficiency, effectiveness and focus in the organization.

The three golden eggs of opportunities that presented themselves to us were hidden in areas that were so conspicuous as to make them nearly invisible. In new and renewal service sales, we found redundancies in the guise of good intentions. Every segment felt their particular situation called for unique processes and workflows when in reality 95 percent of the activities were common across all segments.

In optimizing low-dollar contracts, we leveraged long tail economics. Efficiency and effectiveness opportunities with small contracts that were initially brushed off as "too small to matter" now became a source of substantial value when we considered the quantity of the low dollar contracts.

Finally, as we examined our business from a core vs. context prospective as well as a mission critical vs. non-mission critical perspective, several sweeping improvements became evident. The largest opportunity was in matching personnel skill sets to the complexity and value of activities. This reduced duplication of efforts and better aligned competencies with tasks and reward.

The easiest thing to do is to expound on the rationale of any given change. Rationale, however, only gets you one third of the way there. To engage an organization in change you must also capture their hearts by showing how the changes improve issues they are passionate about. Once you have their heads and hearts you can then enroll their hands by providing activities, tasks and milestones that will move the organization closer to its goal.

We found people were passionate about not wasting time and effort on work that no one really needed or wanted. We also found our staff was passionate about winning. Showing our team that they could win by eliminating valueless activities and by providing space for them to pursue activities our customers and partners valued was the formula for winning. Once the case for change was articulated from a logos as well as pathos perspective, the organization was, at times, eager to commence the transformation journey. There were, of course, obstacles and missteps along the way. In fact, it was much akin to navigating a complex maze called human nature.

The complex maze, labyrinth if you will, was made up of human behaviors, group dynamics and business realities that hounded our every step like the mythical Minotaur. This is not to say the challenges were insurmountable; quite the opposite. We came to understand that change could not happen overnight, that patience and diligence were needed. From a leadership perspective this meant passing the blink test repeatedly; for the organization, it meant getting enough things right to create cultural momentum.

CHAPTER TWELVE

TOOLS OF THE TRADE

My dad used to say, "Kid, every day in every way just try to make yourself a little bit better."[11] This became my mantra in business and in life. As I learned from my systems experience, transformation of any sort will go nowhere without tools to ensure processes are consistent, sticky and transferable. As I worked with my leadership team at Cisco to help lead our organization through transformation, I sought ways to make sure new behaviors were sticking and we had a way of cascading the more pragmatic processes throughout our own teams. I knew we had to keep striving to make ourselves a little better each day and to do that we needed some pragmatic tools.

> *"The leader's job is to set the direction, provide the tools, and then provide the coaching. Some people choose not to take those tools and coaching, and that's okay with them, I suppose, but it's not okay with me."*
>
> —JEFF KANE, SVP, Vantage Data Centers

---

[11] A quote borrowed from Émile Coué (February 26, 1857 – July 2, 1926).

In addition to our work with Larry Liberty we also engaged Mandel Communications. Mandel Communications describe themselves as a "world-class partner for coaching executives, sales, and technical professionals to achieve significantly improved business results through the use of superior communications skills," and they are exactly that. Teaming up with both Liberty and Mandel yielded tools of the trade that we were able to leverage across the organization at all levels as a way to bolster the changes we were trying to make at the leadership level. In this chapter, I will share many of the tools.

MEETING EFFECTIVENESS TOOL

The Meeting Effectiveness Tool emerged from work we were doing to improve communication skills for our sales team. Our sales teams frequently made presentations to both small and large groups, sometimes one on one, sometimes to a room full of people. I wanted to provide our sales team the skills they needed to present with polish and legitimacy whether they were in a boardroom using PowerPoint, in a diner scribbling on a napkin or in an office illustrating on a whiteboard.

We soon realized the tools and techniques we were building had application beyond their original purpose. Our team was not just presenting and communicating with external clients, customers and partners, they were communicating internally with colleagues, managers and senior leaders. As the tool developed, in conjunction with Larry Liberty, we imported it directly into our leadership meetings and from there it quickly cascaded throughout the organization.

The tool walked the users through four steps with four fill-in-the-blank questions as follows:

1. We have _____ minutes for this topic.

2. The end result of our discussion is to _____ (decide / solve / discuss / inform)

3. We would like you to participate by _____. (listening / inquiring / providing expertise / facilitating)

4. Success and effectiveness will be _____.

To reinforce the tool and to help it stick at the leadership team level we started to rate the overall effectiveness of our own meetings. We used a scale of 1-5, with 5 being the highest, and ranked how effective and efficient the meeting was in actualizing the four goals set out in the template. This practice eventually migrated to scoring each presenter so they could get immediate feedback on their presentation efficiency and discussion effectiveness.

SCIPAB®

In addition to the Meeting Effectiveness Tool, we also implemented a communication framework to help staff think through issues and speak succinctly. We developed the framework after I expressed frustration with otherwise bright staff who struggled with presenting requests in a way that would be crystal clear on the problem as well as their request.

Another unproductive time waster was that in meetings, people would tend to save their answer or their request for later in the conversation. Valuable time would evaporate as a meeting meandered back and forth, with people trying to clarify their positions. Ineffective communication can lead to organization wide dysfunction, so I was determined to make my team not just a little better, but much more effective at communications.

I have learned that whether you are having an executive meeting with the C-Suite team or having a conversation with a customer, their "radar" is on from the start of the discussion, quickly scanning for what you want from them: make a decision, spend money, invest resources or just listen. After working with Mandel, we were able to synthesize a tool people could use that would help them articulate their objective in a clear way and frame up a purposeful discussion.

Mandel called the framework SCIPAB, which stands for: Situation, Complication, Implication, Position, Action, and Benefit. My team quickly embraced the model and turned the acronym into a word, pronounced "Sigh-Pab." The Mandel SCIPAB framework walked the user through several stages of critical thinking and forced them to consider the issue from the listener's perspective.

Using the SCIPAB framework quickly advances someone from setting the context to getting right to the point of their core message—stating their position about a recommendation, what needs to happen and how it will benefit the stakeholder. Since the key to SCIPAB is trying to understand the stakeholder's perspective, there is less time spent by each party on positioning. Instead, the stakeholder validates or clarifies the complication and implication presented. If the presenter does their job well, validation of the position and action goes very quickly.

As an example of how SCIPAB flows in narrative, consider the following scenario. A project manager wants to have a discussion with a stakeholder about a recommendation to mitigate some obstacles to delivering a key milestone. Imagine you are that project manager. Using SCIPAB, you might frame your discussion as follows:

> **Stage One:** First, you must realize you are competing with all the other distractions vying for the listener's attention. They may even be in the throes of BADD (business-based attention deficit disorder) behavior. With this in mind, set a compelling context for your topic that is tightly linked to the listener's top concerns. Start by briefly describing the **Situation,** for example a reminder of a project of importance to the listener. Then quickly move on to share the **Complication** that has arisen. This could be a change, challenge or problem that has a negative **Implication** on the results the listener has been counting on for his or her business. The implication is where the rubber hits the proverbial road—if it does not resonate with the listener, as one of their top concerns, there is a good chance the listener will not be paying attention.

> **Stage Two:** If your implication does have "care about value," then the listener will expect to hear your recommendation. Clearly state your **Position**—your high level vision of how to mitigate the problem or act on the opportunity. Then be crystal clear on what specific **Action** you need the listener to take to make your recommendation happen. In order to motivate the listener, describe the **Benefit** of acting on your recommendation, being sure to link those results to the listener's top concerns.

The goal is to create a message that opens the door to a healthy and productive dialogue. That message should be able to be delivered in about two minutes.

My team quickly found that when they used this approach to think through their communications, and especially when they would take a couple of minutes to practice the message prior to the meeting, their discussions (hallway conversations, emails and even voicemails) would progress much more efficiently and productively than normal.

An example of how SCIPAB can work is with the Cisco Services sales transformation I led. In presenting the case for a transformation program, I used the following SCIPAB model to lead the discussion with the Services Executive Council:

The stakes were high because the Services Council would **not** provide funding for sales transformation unless the Sales and Channel Board had our act together—one team, one voice, one plan with all the Sales and Channel global team of leaders dedicated to making it happen.

Situation	Services 2010 is about sales transformation • Sales has grown in complexity with each Theatre having their own sales processes with role clarity, and defined engagement models • Different theatres and different Segments are in different stages of market maturity, market readiness, and critical mass in sales coverage which will result in varying adoption rates of Services 2010
Complication	• Although Services 2010 is a sales-led effort, operational efficiencies are the foundation to achieving the transformation • No one could agree on who or which group (sales vs. ops.) is accountable to drive Services 2010 going forward
Implication	• Without clear alignment & accountability, it will be nearly impossible to drive the sales transformation across Global Operations, Theatre Operations, AS Delivery and AS Operations • Cisco will be unprepared to sell and deliver next-gen solutions to their customers and partners

Needless to say, the approach worked. The beauty of SCIPAB is that it opens the door to a focused, productive dialogue and the entire discussion can usually be resolved in a short amount of time.

Position
To enable Cisco to move into the Solutions via a services-enabled model, Sales will continue to own go to market strategy by Theatre
- Sales and Channels Board should own the execution across all theatres via a project management office (PMO)
- Agree that the PMO will provide guidance & central coordination point for theatres to support the execution of the sales strategy

Action
- Establish a cross functional working group to create the plan for a plan to include WW field sales as well as representatives from AS, TS, and Operations
- Approve a "plan for a plan" to form PMO to help theatres execute sales strategy leveraging Services 2010 global commonalities

Benefit
- Clear accountability of Services 2010 will help accelerate the execution of each Theatre's sales strategy
- Provide Services sales the ability to scale to meet the demands of Cisco's GTM solution sales strategies
- Provide additional Opex to self fund additional Services Transformation

Inside SCIPAB is the principle of "sell the problem, sell the solution." If someone can devise a problem and convince you that it is the cause of all your troubles, then they can sell you a solution. If you really believe in the problem, the solution will actually work!

Imagine the power of a leadership meeting with a maturity factor of adults using SCIPAB and the discussion effectiveness template. Now imagine the power of an entire organization using the same tools surrounded with Level Two communications within a Collaborative Transformation Approach. That was the goal I ultimately had for our organization. I am not suggesting we did all this flawlessly or that within a matter of months the entire Cisco Services sales organization was operating under a new cultural standard. Success using the tools came over time. As it began to work in one corner of the organization, as more and more people embraced the new behaviors and tools, they became true believers and results started to roll in.

SPRING TRAINING

Building high-performing teams, developing leadership and life skills, and creating a culture that retains instead of repelling people takes deliberate effort, creative approaches and pragmatic tools. Back then the idea of services sales was something of a novelty in Cisco. Until then Cisco largely sold boxes and systems and we were moving toward selling service solutions. Even though it was clear that more and more revenue was moving to services and becoming the key to Cisco's long-term growth, the expression "real men only sell iron" was a difficult bias for Cisco to grow out of. Services, for the most part, were an afterthought.

To ensure my team was successful, I needed them to think, act and communicate differently. In addition to working with Mandel and Liberty, I also collaborated closely with our training and development team. With Mandel, we started by building communications 101 skills, including message creation, how to stand, when to pause, how to make eye contact and how to stop saying "uhm." We needed our team to be able to communicate the value and business outcome of our new offerings and solutions in a compelling way that really made sense to our customers and partners. To do this we developed what we called "spring training."

In baseball spring training, players are drilled on the fundamentals of the game. Whether you've been a professional for 5 or 15 years, the first thing they teach you is how to crouch down and catch a ground ball, how to square up on the bat, how to bunt. They go back through all the basics. Our communications curriculum took a similar tact. We decided to develop communications spring training, putting emphasis on how to use nontraditional tools. Nontraditional because we realized if you're an office based employee you tend to make presentations using PowerPoint, but if you present informally you are using a white board, a flip chart, a sheet of paper or a napkin if anything at all.

"I remember after a CXO event the coaches were shaking hands with the presenters after the role playing was over. One of the coaches commented to me, 'Did you notice how sweaty their hands were?'"

—BRAD HOLST, CTO, Mandel Communications

Now, salespeople by nature do not like to practice, yet everyone has to practice somewhere, so it happens in front of the customer. For those sales leaders who are reading this book, ask yourself, "Where do my salespeople practice?" We faced the same problem. Once spring training was clipping along well, we wanted to create an opportunity for our staff to use and practice their skills outside of a classroom setting. We wanted the skills we taught to be "sticky," to last more than that one day of training and take root so deeply that the skills would be used intuitively on an ongoing basis.

To meet this goal we took what was traditionally a classroom experience and added the pressure of the pipeline freeze by bringing in retired and current executive mentors, real CXO's (CIO, CTO, COO, etc.) from some of our existing customers. We developed a training class around real world role-plays using real world executives. Much to our pleasant surprise, we found our customers were happy to commit their time. Quite simply, they wanted to help Cisco be successful in meeting their needs.

To truly create stickiness in our communications training, we capped the experience with a fun, competitive event that provided an ample reward for the top ranking performers. We put together competitions at the region, operation and segment level with winners at each level getting cash awards and advancing to finals in San Jose where senior and executive vice presidents served as judges. Talk about the "pucker" factor! Not only were the folks in the competition performing in front of their peers but in front of the top leadership of the company! It was a great way to differentiate the high flyers, high potentials and those who could use more development.

We formalized the competition into what we called Making the Executive Connection (MEC). That was the first year. The next year we upgraded *Making the Executive Connection* to *Making the Partner Connection*. We knew that not only do Cisco salespeople talk to customers, but their customers may in fact be the partner, because 86% of our business goes through the channel partners. We took an extensible methodology and were able to make it applicable to more audiences just by reframing the questions, restating the outcome. We also added a public sector version where we brought in people from government to participate.

> *"After the CXO competition was completed there were two types of comments you'd hear: 'You really get to see the top performers in action' and 'I thought my people were better than that.'"*
>
> —DOUG DENNERLINE, CEO, SuccessFactors

Communications hinge on our ability to connect. Connecting depends as much on how we communicate as well as what we communicate. Message delivery has to be as good as the content itself; in fact, how the message is delivered is an integral part of the message itself. Through our spring training, the follow on competitions, and the subsequent behavioral and cultural changes we effected, the business skills advantage we leveraged became a new set of communication muscles. The life skills advantage we leveraged was to enable our staff to more authentically connect with their colleagues as well as people in other facets of their lives.

If you cannot say it and you cannot communicate it, you are less effective or less influential in business and in life. In the workplace, your seat at the table gets smaller and smaller. In life, your span of influence shrinks and shrinks.

PAPA'S GOT A BRAND NEW BAG

Increasing your ability to communicate and connect will make you a stronger, more effective leader. The skills we taught in our spring training and CXO competition helped to embed those abilities and make them stick, but I needed more practice and reinforcement for my leadership team and I needed it to take place in their everyday workflow. I turned to a new style of executive coaching.

Traditional executive coaching focuses on a few key behaviors to change or improve. The executive coach says, "You need to be more assertive in meetings." Generally, that coaching is done on the phone. It is rarely face-to-face. A typical executive coach comes up and says "you need to be more assertive," then six weeks goes by and they say, "Well, what happened in the last six weeks?"

The coach tells the mentee "what" needs to be done in general terms while making a few suggestions, but does not actually help with execution. To change this dynamic we used Mandel Communications coaches to work with my staff in their everyday activities, to observe their communication skills and to use proven communication techniques to help modify the mentee's behavior. By focusing on real execution we increased the stickiness of executive coaching.

ONCE UPON A TIME

The power of storytelling has been gaining momentum as a change management and communication tool for some time now. The reality is, of course, that storytelling is as old as language and has always been one of the most powerful communication practices in existence. At its core, a story is a way to convey information to increase understanding of a topic, event or even process. People are more interested in stories than in pure information. Stories, then, become a way to package information in a compelling way. Human beings have a natural attraction to stories, and, as it turns out, most people have a natural inclination to tell them. The trick is, of course, to tell them well.

There is a lot of noise in the world today, call it "data," and stories make sense out of all that data. They also focus on the human element. In a sense, stories take data, wrap it up in human elements—point of view, conflict, emotion, resolution, reversals—and allow the recipients to absorb the information in way that is interesting and memorable. Given the unfathomable sea of information in the world today, storytelling is an invaluable resource for delivering substance and meaning in a form that can be readily grasped by others.

In transforming the Services sales organization at Cisco, I sought to tap into the power of storytelling by having my leaders hone their own storytelling skills.

With the help of Brad Holst at Mandel, we developed a storyteller framework to help our sales team more effectively communicate, collaborate and sell with their internal key stakeholders and external customers. The framework helped them to use stories to introduce concepts, to clarify points in my presentations and to build relationships. An additional benefit to storytelling is the extra horsepower it can lend to problem solving. Stories certainly help others to understand what you need to get across, but in creating stories out of raw information, you are also able to view a problem or situation better, thus enabling you to arrive at a more effective solution. Sometimes the data is overwhelming, but the story behind the spreadsheet can be illuminating for both the receiver and the sender.

There is a science to storytelling. In creating our framework, Brad Holst leveraged the time proven methodology of "classical storytelling" by putting a fresh spin on it in order to make it simple, intuitive and memorable. I should note here that he quickly dispelled the bad memories of any high school English class where stories were discussed in dry clinical terms like protagonist and antagonist.

Now, "classical storytelling" predates human use of written language and is used in every culture from the most advanced to the most primitive. Multiple research studies suggest that human beings are naturally hard wired to receive information in this format. The storyteller framework has four components:

1. **Once upon a time...** There is a reason why good, repeatable stories often start with some form of that classic fairy tale opening. To engage with the story, the listener wants a setting they can identify with and a hero they can relate to and care about. Stories about people—people that the storyteller gets the listener to care about—are exponentially more engaging than stories about faceless corporations and products.

2. **There was a shark!** Stories about everything going right are BORING. There needs to be some kind of inciting incident that sets the story in motion by putting the hero in some sort of jeopardy. Mandel calls this a "shark." If one shark is good, then following with more sharks are even better. Listeners love to hear about problems and challenges, even to the point where there is what professional screenwriters refer to as "a whiff of death."

3. **And they all lived happily ever after...Or maybe they did not.** Stories become memorable when they have a believable yet unpredictable ending—predictability also equals BORING. Events need to build up that bring the story to resolution, which could be a happy conclusion where everything comes together for the hero, or it could be a cautionary tale where lessons are learned when the shark wins.

4. **What is your point?** This is the reason why a story was told in the first place. Having listened and engaged with the story, the listener now expects the storyteller to share the lesson learned and make the call to action. If the storyteller has done a good job the storyteller has earned the right to make his or her point.

> *"We needed to crack the code as most virtual training was like having leg hair pulled out one at a time."*
>
> —BRAD HOLST, CTO, Mandel Communications

There is also an art to storytelling. The leader who effectively uses stories to influence others must practice those stories until they have a muscle memory feel to them, allowing the leader spin the same story multiple ways depending on the listener and the situation. They polish their stories until they can be told in two minutes or less in most circumstances–brevity is critical as human attention spans are short and getting shorter all the time. Leaders who use stories successfully fully commit to the telling of the story, going all in with descriptive word choices and an authentic delivery that leverages their natural vocal qualities, facial expressions, gestures and use of pauses to bring their stories to life for their listeners.

Because of this investment, the natural storytellers on my team found that by learning how to tell stories correctly they improved the emotional connection with their listeners, and they made their key messages much more memorable. The results were even more dramatic with the people who would describe themselves as "not a storyteller." These were often strong analytical thinkers who, once given a framework, found that they could get the same benefit and results as the natural storytellers.

Many people believe they are good storytellers, but what most call storytelling is the retelling of an event as opposed to aligning with the message and content you want to convey to the audience. I thought I was good at telling humorous stories or using analogies to paint pictures and war stories of success as a point of reference. However, learning how to tell stories correctly allowed me to improve the emotional connection with the listener, helped the audience remember the key messages and helped me to realize that it is a lot more fun to **tell stories** than to **talk at** people.

COLLABORATION "R" US

During my time at Cisco, we did something called "Cisco on Cisco." Cisco faces many of the same business and IT challenges as their customers do. Our goal was to build use cases based upon the practical experience and lessons learned deploying Cisco products and technologies internally. Many sales leaders experience major discomfort or awkwardness with new communication technologies. As a result, sometimes leaders unintentionally keep new communications technologies away from their team.

When the bottom fell out in 2008/09, Cisco stopped all travel unless it was for customer or partner business visits. Therefore, to accomplish skills development training, we needed to leverage the robust set of Cisco's collaborative toolkit. I challenged my learning partner, Mandel Communications, to crack the code on how to deliver virtual training that could accomplish two things that most training vendors at the time found impossible to do: engage and hold the short attention spans of the sales team, again, breaking the dysfunction of BADD (business-based attention deficit disorder), and deliver real behavior change.

Mandel, who until then had always delivered training face to face, rose to the challenge and went into deep research and development mode. First, they delivered a world-class webinar at a virtual all-hands meeting that not only received great reviews, but also demonstrated what was possible in the virtual presentation environment. Mandel then went on to deliver highly interactive virtual workshops that even, to their surprise, nearly matched the results of their face-to-face work with my team. They expanded their offerings to include workshops on communicating virtually as well as conducting coaching over the virtual medium. Other training providers at Cisco, not wanting to be left behind, upped their game and started to deliver much improved virtual workshops and seminars.

From this experience we quickly learned that not only were these collaboration tools great to deliver training and host internal meetings, we also found them to be very effective to collaborate with customers virtually via WebEx, then TelePresence and then TelePresence enabled WebEx sessions. They proved invaluable in delivering our service solutions to customers and partners as well.

Embracing and mastering the use of virtual collaboration technology proved to be an accelerator for my transformation strategy. It did not replace business travel all together, as face-to-face time is critical to relationship building, but it reduced travel while enabling an increase in customer intimacy and boosted collaboration levels internally. It makes me shudder to think what would have happened if I had let my sales teams' and my training partners' discomfort with these invaluable collaboration technologies prevent their productive adoption. That is a sad tale that has brought down many otherwise high functioning organizations. Most human beings, unless prodded and motivated, will never leave their comfort zone.

COMPLACENCY BREEDS MEDIOCRITY

I firmly believe that to help people grow and develop you need to get them out of their comfort zones to learn new behaviors required to reach the next level. A comfort zone can be defined as conditioning that causes a person to operate inside self-imposed mental boundaries. Highly successful people routinely step outside their comfort zones to accomplish what they wish. For me there are two comfort zone challenges: one is communication, the other risk.

Comfort Zone 1: Your potential as a genuine and authentic communicator is much greater than your current communication comfort zone. A key trait of great communicators, the ones that really connect with and inspire their listeners, is that they engage with their audience in a wholly genuine and authentic manner. In short, they are very good at being themselves. While this should be a helpful observation for those aspiring to be great communicators, there is also a risk if taken too literally it could be an excuse for not achieving one's full communication potential by saying: "Hey, that's just how I am." When we say that, what we are really saying is, "Hey, that's just my comfort zone." There is a big difference between what is in the realm of communication skills that we are comfortable with and those outside our comfort zone yet still within our reach.

You need to experiment with new and different behaviors before you can experience the new results they generate. This requires self-awareness, conscious effort and practice, and taking risk.

> *"It's not fun when you're having complacency shaken out of you and you are forced to reach your full potential. It's a journey, and not always an enjoyable one, but when you get to the end you think, 'Okay, well, I expanded my comfort zone.' Yeah, and you're going to do it again and again. It takes awhile to realize that. Now I know why George did all this over the years."*
>
> —CORINN HASTINGS, Chief of Staff, Cisco Systems

Comfort Zone 2: When it comes to risk, most people do not know their own physical or mental limits. Getting people outside their comfort zones can be scary for them. In the end, however, people realize that once they are outside of their comfort zone, it is not so bad. Actually, it usually feels worse getting there than being there. For my purposes, I tried to find ways to encourage people and reward them to step out of their comfort zones, to stretch themselves and take a risk.

Move yourself farther out than where your team is. A leader needs to create space and then let others step into the space they used to occupy.

One of the keys to selling is taking risk out of the decision. Apply that to comfort zones. By giving people encouragement to stretch and then giving them tools of the trade, the risk became less adverse. You can be the General Colin Powell leader who says, "We're going to take Hill 405," but unless you take the time to give the troops the necessary training, the skills, the tactics and the strategies to pull that off then it seems like a hill too far. If you give people the correct tools, the communications skills, the ability to handle objections, then when they get into the heat of battle and they get outside their comfort zone, their chances of success go up immensely. That is the science piece to it. Once they start to do it more and more often, it becomes an art form.

Leaders have to give their managers the choice to become a leader or to sit back as a manager and say, "Tell me where to go and what to do coach."

The tools of the trade help transform a team by coaxing them to get a little better every day in every way. The trick is to transform while life is in full motion. Transformation in motion can only be done in practical small steps or "micro moments." Micro moments are a series or collection of positive experiences. You can create micro moments by enabling people with the tools, role-playing, and practice so they have first-hand experience of the new behaviors and are then able to replicate the "stories" in real time with their customers/prospects. When the troops change, the results will change as well.

In my experience with the Cisco Services sales organization we did more than address the typical technical skills training. We focused on communication and connection skills. We provided real tools people could use every day, not only in the workplace but in their lives. We dared to improve life skills in the business arena. People are scared to death to do that. They are afraid it will make them seem weak as leaders. The truth is, developing people in ways that transcend the workplace delivers business performance and much more. It delivers a corporate brand people want to be part of; it creates a culture of productivity and results.

Specific tools we leveraged were: the Meeting Effectiveness Tool, SCIPAB, Communications Spring Training, non-traditional executive coaches, storytelling and collaboration technologies. These tools worked for the specific situation my team faced. Each leader should carefully assess the needs of their teams before trialing their own tools. The common factor across the tools was that they were all communications related. For us, communications made up a large part of the leadership gap. We found as we improved in these areas, we transformed across the board.

It takes less time for an individual to go through transformation than for an entire organization. The good thing is it gives you as the leader an opportunity to make that change yourself and to be a role model for others. When they see you as the leader making the change, when they see you advancing, when they see you as a true leader, then you can start your work. In the next section, we will explore what personal transformation entails.

SECTION V

TRANSFORMING FROM WITHIN

"Becoming a leader is synonymous with becoming yourself. It is precisely that simple, and it is also that difficult."

—WARREN G. BENNIS

CHAPTER THIRTEEN

THE FENG SHUI OF LEADERSHIP

The communication bar is set high at Cisco when you have John Chambers as CEO. When I was with Cisco, every executive was measured on how well they performed in front of large audiences at strategic leadership meetings, key off-sites, annual sales and partner conferences, even presentations at our Executive Briefing Center. At his quarterly executive staff meetings, John would review how many executive briefings each one of us held and how we were rated on the customer surveys (1 being low and 5 being high) which the Briefing Center staff conducted. You did not want to see your name with very few briefings or a score lower than 4.3 (5.0 was the benchmark). Everyone was motivated to improve their communication skills across the board, and I was no exception.

Until this point, I learned a lot about communications from Mandel and other communication consultants, such as Loraine Antrim with Core Ideas Communication. I felt, however, that I needed some further development. In fact, Ian Griffin, my executive communications manager, suggested I needed to work on reducing my Chicago accent. I should say my view was that Ian needed to work on his British hearing, but that is another story. I took his advice and began to work with a communications coach from Orange County, CA. Her name is Kate Peters. Kate identifies herself as a vocal impact communications coach and author, but she is much more. What she has taught me is this: To effectively influence an audience, a speaker needs to identify their intention as a communicator, and the intention needs to be germane and authentic to the speaker; then the speaker needs to align his or her message with that intention; the message, in turn, needs to be aligned with his or her delivery.

You will be delegated to whom you sound like. If you want to have an executive discussion, then your intention and communication style has to match an executive audience.

This chain of congruence may sound simple but each nugget carries volumes of import, not least of which is the concept of "intention." As Kate worked with me to make me a better speaker, as she kept probing at this idea of intention, I realized what she was getting at wasn't just presentation skills, it was a deep leadership principle that most leaders play on the fringes of but rarely put into action.

The beauty of Kate's approach was that she started fine-tuning the small but critical stuff. These included delivery-oriented techniques such as breathing control, intonation, inflection, articulation and much more to strengthen my delivery and align my vocal image with how I wanted to be perceived. At the starting point of these techniques, however, was one enabling question. Kate would ask me repeatedly, day after day, "George, what's your intention?" I would answer with something like, "I want to encourage my audience to take xyz action" or "I want to drive engagement in xyz strategy." She would nod her head and say something encouraging like, "Excellent, George, that's good" and then follow it with, "Now I want you to really think about what your intention is. George, what is your intention?"

As I continued my work with Kate, it became clear to me what she was driving at was not the micro-intention of a presentation but a macro-intention of what was behind the presentation. How did my intention for leading or speaking align with the way others heard from me and what they saw in me? Was it aligned or was there confusion? If I communicated a mixed message, I would lose credibility. This led me to consider the overarching strategy I was trying to communicate, how I was communicating it and, more importantly, what was I doing to make sure that strategy aligned end-to-end, both as a business plan and as a leadership imperative.

If strategy provides focus, then focus provides intention. I came to understand that there has to be a focus that guides action, and focus applied consistently in conversation, in presentation, in behavior, in strategy, in business, defines our intention. Taken further, intention needs to be clear and deliberate rather than an afterthought. Although deliberate by definition, intention is often incidental in action. Many leaders think they know their intention, but instead it is an objective, vision or goal they have in mind.

Intention is an aim that guides action, not just a goal.

From my experience, incidental intention leads to ambiguity and frustration in an organization. We see this in so many businesses today. I learned a long time ago that part-time effort (or intention) delivers part-time results. Likewise, unidentified intention can also be dangerous. For example, if you have to fire someone and you set your intention no further than a friendly discussion, you have not really been honest about your intention and the conversation could be disastrous, never getting to the point or with the termination coming as a huge surprise to the person you need to fire. It would be better to acknowledge the intention to let them go, and include the intention to move them along with dignity and respect.

SAY WHAT YOU MEAN, MEAN WHAT YOU SAY

Kate Peters' method—alignment of intention—is like the Feng Shui of leadership. Intention when applied in leadership allows a leader's personality, the human side of what they do and who they are, to come through as part of his or her communication. I learned the more precise your intention, the better your connection will be with the listener, audience or company. Since intention is an art and not a science, everyone's intention shows up differently. Our intention, then, is like a fingerprint. If you think about how leadership impacts a business, the idea of a leader's fingerprints being left on an organization becomes more than a simple truism, it becomes a fact.

An interesting thing about intention is how quickly its alignment or misalignment is evident to others. In the first 30 seconds of speaking to someone they make a judgment about who you are based on bits of evidence that come through about your education, your upbringing, your role and many other distinguishing factors. These bits of information are transmitted in the way we present ourselves, from our vocal image to our physical appearance. For instance, a leader who has poor diction and articulation, and who speaks too fast and appears nervous, is not going to align well with a message of excellence and trust. In fact, if such a leader were to try to deliver a message of excellence and trust, the sheer incongruence of his or her intention would undermine them within seconds. That is not to say it would stop them. In fact, they would likely continue in their incongruence, sending mixed messages and causing confusion. For instance, if you are running late for an appointment on a busy day, you may rush through a budget presentation, giving the impression that the subject is not important to you. You may think your intention is about reviewing the budget and agreeing interventions, but your real intent may be to get to your next appointment. Your audience is going to read mixed signals and misunderstand what you were actually driving at.

On the surface, alignment of delivery, message and intention denotes authenticity and genuineness. "No one is going to believe a word you say," Kate told me, "unless what you say lines up with how you say it and how you say it lines up with what you really seem to be pushing for." For me this lesson was reflected in a number of my past experiences. I will share two with you here. One shows the power of aligned intention, the other the power of misaligned intention.

MY SON HAS TATTOOS

Earlier in my tenure with Cisco, I was the executive sponsor for our Toronto Dominion (TD) Bank customer. I had an appointment, my first call actually, with the Chief Information Officer (CIO). Unfortunately, at the last minute the CIO canceled. Luckily, the senior account manager was able to land us another appointment. This one was with the Executive Vice President (EVP) of retail banking, the person who oversaw all the retail branches for TD Bank in Canada and North America.

We had 30 minutes, and I was told he was as hard as nails. "If he senses you aren't worth the time, he's going to kick you out in the first 15 minutes," the senior account manager told me in a two-minute curbside briefing. I felt like I was back on the football field with the coach telling me not to worry, "but the game is in your hands, now go back out there and score a touchdown!"

As I walked into the EVP's office, I'll call him Brian, I started looking for the beautiful clock. Sure enough, there was a picture of two young men on his credenza in hockey uniforms. I said, "Brian, these are your two sons? Wow, they must be good hockey players." His face lit up.

"Well, yeah," he said and went on to share a story about their latest game.

We then started to talk about business. Since Brian owned the entire Bank's retail relationships, I asked how they measured customer satisfaction.

"Well, George it's funny you ask," Brian replied. "The CEO and I were out in Ottawa a few weeks ago. We were out in the branches doing mini focus groups. We were going up to customers as they left the bank. 'So Dave, why do you do business at TD Bank?' And the resounding answer, get this, the most common answer that came back from the customers was 'because you look like us. Your tellers, your platform officers, they look like us. They have buzz cuts, they have tattoos; they have earrings like us. We see ourselves when we come into your banks, so we feel at home.'"

A little more at ease, he invited us to sit down. I took that opportunity to open up. I told him, "I have two sons as well. One of the things that keeps me awake at night," I said, "what scares me is they're about to enter the workforce. I don't know about you, but what do you think about kids today and some of the things they do? One of my sons happens to have a couple tattoos on his arm." I noticed he was listening intently. He might have been expecting some sort of sales pitch, but instead what he was getting was a two-minute check-in from a guy he had only just met.

I continued, "That's going to be a little career limiting for my kid, but it gives me hope knowing there are organizations like yours they could work for."

Ten minutes into the appointment and he and I are exchanging stories about our sons that are leading into insights about culture. We got there because I took a chance and put myself out there. I disclosed that I had a son who had tattoos and that I that did not know what to think about it. Here was this senior vice president from Cisco disclosing something personal, being vulnerable to an executive vice president of a major bank. That was a Level 2 conversation enabled by trust and transparency. In the next 20 minutes we went into how Cisco technologies and services were something they should invest in. Fast forward a few quarters and we ran a small trial; fast forward two years, 25 TelePresence systems, 77,000 phones and two new data centers later, and we are still sharing stories about our sons and the worries and joys that come with them. That is the power of relationships that is the power of authenticity and trust.

MICRO-INEQUITIES

Just as authentic communications can build trust, so miscommunications from misaligned intention can break down trust. The scary thing is that misaligned intention can and does happen in small ways every day unless we are vigilant. These misalignments are called micro-inequities.

One of my early managers, who was a great influence on me in terms of what it means to be a salesperson, had a trait that for some reason I was always enamored with. He would have sales team meetings where he would update us on the latest strategy coming out of head office. He would read the notices and as he finished each one, he would tear them in half and drop them into the trashcan behind him or if the wastebasket were too far away, he would crumple the memo and then attempt to be Michael Jordan and nail a 3-pointer. I saw it as simply as I think he meant it—memo read, message absorbed, team aligned.

So there I was at Cisco just two years into my job. Many people would come by my office from marketing, operations, and other departments to present work and ideas. One morning a manager, her name was Rita, came by and presented a proposal to me. It was very straightforward and made perfect sense. I got the message, decided I would follow up on it and put it right into practice. As Rita left my office, I said, "thank you very much for coming in" and then I took her printed report, tore it in half and dropped it in the trashcan (just like my old manager would have done). I did this subconsciously; it just happened. For me it meant we made a decision and the meeting over. At least that is what I thought I was saying. I had picked up this practice some 25+ years before then, and there it was resurfacing. This demonstrates how lasting these latent influences can be.

A few weeks later, I attended what we called a "micro-inequities" training as part of a larger inclusion and diversity campaign. Micro-inequities is about the "micro messages" you send with your actions and what may happen when those messages do not align with your intentions. As I went through the training, it suddenly struck me. I thought, "Holy crap!" What I had intended by tearing up Rita's report and what I had probably conveyed were miles apart. I went back and asked Rita's boss to find out how she felt about our meeting. He told me she was devastated because in her eyes I took her best work and threw it away in front of her. I apologized to Rita. My lesson that day was that when our actions do not seem to align with our intent, they can have quite the opposite effect.

That story was actually written up in a Cisco Inclusion and Diversity publication. It was seen as a powerful story; firstly, because I was willing to admit to it. Second, because it was such a perfect example of unintentional micro-inequities that can carry so much unspoken weight.

STRATEGIC INTENTION

The two stories above demonstrate how intention can impact one-on-one communications. Stories like these kept rolling through my mind as Kate and I worked on an overall strategic intention for my communication that would inspire me as well as others. Intuitively I knew what communication intent looked and felt like; I just needed to crystallize it in a cohesive statement, one that captured what I believed in and how I wanted to influence others. After some work and careful reflection, I came up with the following: "I want to be a deliberate, purposeful communicator, who can throw his heart over an obstacle and have others follow."

As my intention of communication became evident to me, other stars started to line up as well. I realized that Kate was coaching me about intention as a means to connect with an audience, be it a group or an individual, and this was much bigger than presentation skills or any other communication tactics. If the idea of intention could be applied to communication, what could be accomplished by applying it to strategy and business?

We can define strategic intention for a business or enterprise as a compelling statement that answers the question:"What exactly are we trying to accomplish?" When I thought of my experience with Cisco, that question was easy to answer. It was there in everything we did from VSE to teamwork-and-collaboration to how I wanted my leaders to be a high performing team. I saw that the importance of strategic intent for a business was not simply in articulating it, but in consistently bringing it to life in everything thing an organization did. It had to become a core element in the DNA of the organization.

Like intention of communication, the power of strategic intention comes in alignment. Strategic intention has to be the leadership mantra that an organization rallies around.

When applied consistently by leaders in words and actions, in vision, strategy and execution, when institutionalized through tools, practices and processes, when infused in an organization's culture, "aligned strategic intention" will bring about a virtuous cycle of results that cannot be stopped.

Aligned strategic intention in a business builds the future based upon the future. It enables the ability to see the potential of the present from the point of view of the future. However, to do this, leaders must learn to communicate using skills that are deliberate, challenging and inclusive. Leaders have to communicate—and not just by talking but by truly listening—with authenticity, clarity, transparency, and integrity. Here again I will emphasize that all of this starts from inside a leader. A leader cannot hope to instill a strategic intention upon a business without first coming to terms with his or her own personal strategic intention.

AN INTENTIONAL LIFE

I absolutely believe everyone should have a personal strategic intention they use to guide their way in life. Personal strategic intention should express the essence of and passion you have for life, whether it's for winning, accomplishing, achieving, leading, loving, sharing, growing—whatever it is, it should be compelling, it should call to you and touch you deeply. It should inspire you to get up every morning to pursue it and keep you up at night when it's eluding you. Personal strategic intention should answer the question: What do I want to be? And it should be expressed as broadly as possible.

To wax philosophical for a moment, I believe our personality and being are formed early on. I also believe that while the tracks of our life have been laid out, they can also be shifted. We are who we are, and we must strive to mature, develop, correct and adjust who we are as best as we can for the benefit of ourselves and those around us—family, friends, colleagues, customers. Life is an opportunity and what we do with that opportunity is too important and precious to waste.

Maybe the ability to understand and grasp the power of intention as it applies to communication, to business, to life, is directly tied to the leadership gene. Maybe it is not evident for everyone but just bubbles up as an inert need. Maybe that is why people go to church and believe in a higher power and the resulting connected experience of a shared intention. Maybe the need for intention is a natural, universal facet of the human condition.

Maybe's aside, a well-lived life requires awareness, it requires deliberate focus, and yes, it requires intention. Many people go through life just bumping into circumstance by accident, leaving their path open to happenstance and the plans of others. They just go along for the ride. Sometimes that ride is good and sometimes it is bad. The truly sad thing is this: If you live your life without intention, it is like my dad used to say, "Either you have a plan or you are part of someone else's plan."

INSTANT REPLAY

A mature adult, a good communicator, a strong leader has to be authentic in what he or she says and does. That authenticity is measured by alignment with intention and results in trust. It's the Feng Shui of leadership. Aligned, authentic communications as a way to build trust is not just a parlor trick for the boardroom; it is a way of life. Authenticity, aligning your intent with your actions and your words, happens in all moments, especially during a blink test. As leaders, we are always on stage and that stage is called life.

Aligned intention is a powerful leadership principle that has application in all communication, business and in life. The reality is, to apply intention to only one or two of these areas is a matter of science. Applying it to all three is a matter of art.

Just as aligned intention can have tremendous positive effects, even the smallest of misaligned intentions can have dramatic negative effects. While it may be easy to anticipate and avoid major misalignments, it's the micro-inequities that can easily catch you unaware. Micro-inequities occur when we unknowingly play out learned biases or behaviors that may seem innocent enough to us in the moment but may be devastating to others. The only way to avoid micro-inequities is to be keenly aware of your actions as well as your words and carefully consider their impact. As you deliberately align your actions and words with your communications intention, there will be less opportunity for major and minor mishaps, such as micro-inequities. Remember, everything a leader does communicates.

While examining all your communicative actions, words and behaviors may seem overwhelming, the best place to start is by being clear and honest with yourself. Without clarity there can be no honesty. Many people seem to convey misaligned intention because they simply don't know their own intentions. They come across as mistrustful. Before you can successfully convince your organization to line up behind you or beside you, they first must trust you. That, my friends, is something you cannot fake.

Once you become practiced in aligning your communications intention, you can then work on aligning your strategic intention. Aligning your communications intention is about matching your actions, words and behaviors to your motivation. Strategic intent is aligning all those instances across a continuum, showing consistency and a clear trajectory toward a coherent goal. Aligned strategic intention should not only net a leader the trust of his or her organization, it should also net remarkable business results.

CONCLUSION

LIVING A LEGACY

Our personal intention gives purpose and meaning to our lives. When applied consistently in business, a strategic intention flows through the systems, processes and people that make up the organization. In this way intention comes to life in tangible results that can make a powerful impact on a wide variety of stakeholders, from employees to clients to shareholders to customers. The imprint our intention leaves on the world, on people, on organizations, is our legacy. Intention is the aim that guides action; legacy is the mark that action leaves. And just as intention is a wine best served with deliberate purpose, so should legacy be aligned with purpose and a personal vision. In this way, personal vision, aligned with action, leaves a legacy.

As I started to step through the process of first defining my communication intention, then clarifying my strategic intention and finally considering my own personal intention, I was confronted again with the question of legacy, something I had considered in my early days at Cisco. I recall the day it happened.

FOR WHAT IT'S WORTH

I joined Cisco in June of 2000 as a vice president. The crash happened in February of 2001. At the end of the fourth quarter of 2001 I was wondering, "What's this all about?" A lot of people had lost their jobs and their fortunes due to the crash, so I felt blessed I was still employed and Cisco was financially stable. At the time the role of senior vice president was my next logical career move. As I considered the role, I observed many senior vice presidents who had succeeded in advancing their careers. I also observed what it took to be a senior vice president. I observed readily that I would have to sell another piece of my soul, of my life, and I wanted to understand if it was worth it.

To help me wrestle with this question and to further develop my leadership skills I hired an executive coach. I have noted earlier that some people believe having a coach is like the scarlet letter, but it really is a badge of courage because it shows you want to improve yourself. You should never be ashamed of recognizing you can improve.

My executive coach worked with me in a number of ways. One particularly powerful thing she did was to have me do an interview version of a 360 feedback loop. The results confirmed some of my beliefs and revealed some of my blind spots. As we reviewed the results and discussed actions I could take, I felt it was time to share the dilemma I had been struggling with. She had coached numerous vice presidents, senior vice presidents and even CEO's. I felt more than comfortable with expressing to her my uncertainty about a senior vice president role and whether or not it was worth the sacrifice.

What she taught me was the interview question I am so fond of today. She said, "George, let me ask you this question: When it's time for you to leave Cisco, what do you want your legacy to be?"

My answer was that I wanted to leave Cisco having helped the organization move from selling boxes to selling systems to selling solutions and having built the organization, the relationships, the capabilities and the mindsets to make sure Cisco could continue to be successful long into the future.

She then asked the follow-up question which I have since used in many coaching situations. She said, "Okay, George, if that's going to be your legacy, would becoming a senior vice president help you achieve it?"

I thought about it and then responded: "Yes, it would give me a bigger venue, more opportunity to influence and a broader stage to play on, which would help me meet my personal legacy. So, yes, becoming a senior vice president would help me to achieve my legacy." Things became a lot clearer then.

Here's what I learned: When someone gets clear on their legacy, and they tie that to what they strive to achieve every day in the workplace, you have to start telling them to stop working, to go home, to take vacations, to go see their families. And that's the secret to leadership. If you can align people's intentions for their personal and professional life to the work they do, to the outcomes of what they want their legacy to be, that is when you see leaders, companies, teams, and organizations producing extraordinary results.

Many people aspire to an altruistic legacy of being known as a solid citizen who made a difference, who made an impact and who helped develop people. If that's truly the legacy that somebody wants to be remembered for, if that's ultimately the horizon that's part of their fulfillment, then moving up the chain of command really is not that important, because you can mentor, coach, develop and have just as much influence on that legacy as an individual contributor as you can as a director or a vice president. This fact surprises many people because the corporate work ethic says climb, climb, and climb. The truth is, climbing the chain of command is good from an economic standpoint, but you can be incredibly fulfilled in a lower level role actualizing an altruistic legacy. Think of the many people who have climbed the corporate ladder and reaped financial rewards only to be miserable because they missed fulfilling their legacy.

BACK TO THE FUTURE

Here is a curious twist to legacies: When we talk about legacies, it is usually in the past tense. Thinking about legacies in the past tense is a case of too little too late. Paradoxically, legacies are not about the past, they are about the future.

I talk about my dad a lot. I recall once we were visiting a gravesite of someone who had was very special to both of us. He said, "George, when you die, you want people to be able to look at your tombstone, and say here lies the sum total of George O'Meara. You have to think about that and figure out how to live while there is still time." I don't know if I said it then because I was still processing it and I still had so much to learn, but I'll say it now, "Thank you Dad."

Now almost 35 years later I think back on those words. What strikes me is that it is too late to think about your legacy when your time is up, and not just in the sense of life in general. It is too late to think about the legacy you want to leave a company when you are in the process of walking out of the front door of the office for that last time. The time to think about your legacy is now.

As I look back on my career, I ask myself, "Have I fulfilled my legacy?"

To answer properly I have to examine the question a little more deeply. I have purposefully left off a qualifier that would suggest a legacy in the workplace vs. a legacy in my personal life. In taking assessments like the Myers Briggs Type Indicator, Predictive Index, or DiSC, many people will ask: Should I answer these questions based on who I am at work or who I am at home? That has always struck me as an odd and potentially dangerous notion. It seems to me that compartmentalizing ourselves can lead to bad things. I have always been a proponent of a single self—essentially; you should show up in the workplace the same way you show up at home. Segmenting yourself will burn off a lot of necessary energy and will create threads that will be difficult to keep untangled. For me, I want my legacy to span all of who I am. My legacy is not tied just to a career or a lifestyle; it is what I want to do with all of my life, not just compartments of my life.

The fact that the question is written in the past tense brings up the notion of *when* a legacy should be established. Personally, I think a person's intended legacy can and should change over time. It changes as we mature as adults; it changes as we experience the hardships and blessings of life; it changes as our perspective of the world changes. I am not sure I would want to be held to my college day version of my legacy. I'm certain it had something to do with a Chevelle SS 396, playing some form of sports and having more money than I could ever use—all of which I have grown out of desiring (well, maybe not the Chevelle). I would also say there would probably be some enduring aspects of a legacy I might have formed as a young adult in college that I would still want as part of my legacy today. A legacy of friends and family, both with which I have been amply blessed, come to mind. All this is to say, legacies are not static. Just as we grow and develop, so should our legacies grow and develop.

The last nuance I will touch on is the idea of when a legacy is deemed completed. As I described earlier, a legacy should be underpinned with actions, behaviors and words that are aligned to a single purpose. As I progress through each day, I strive to keep my own actions, behaviors and words aligned as I work toward the goal of leaving my legacy.

If I pause here a moment and reflect on the most rewarding aspect of playing sports, I'd have to say that it is *playing* the game as opposed to *winning* the game. It is always great to win, but if that is all you want, then you will miss the real pleasure that sports have to offer—and that is the sheer pleasure of playing the game to begin with. My point is simple: "I do not intend to **leave** a legacy; I intend to **live** a legacy." My question to you, my reader, is *what do you want your legacy to be?*

AFTERWORD

When I started writing this book I had the intention of leaving a legacy, not only for myself as a reminder of the things which I was most proud of achieving in the business world, but also as a MacGyver-like tool for up and coming leaders. I wanted to say, "Hey, I learned some things along the way that were instrumental in helping me succeed, and I think they will really help you along your way. Let me help. Let me share my lessons."

As I started the book, I had some very clear ideas of what those lessons were. In retracing my steps from individual contributor to manager to leader; in interviewing colleagues and mentors about the themes in this book; in remembering and recounting my history and the history of those around me; I rediscovered insights I had left just below the surface of my consciousness. These are insights that I am still able to access in my everyday efforts to be a stronger leader and better person. Perhaps it is the reflective nature of writing, perhaps it is the act of focused thinking; either way, I discovered and rediscovered things about leadership that had not been top of mind the first day I sat at the keyboard.

The writing of this book has been a journey, a journey I am glad I have taken and, indeed, a journey that I am glad that you, dear reader, have joined. It is for you, after all, that I wrote this book.

If there are three final things I would impart, they are:

- **"Know thyself,"** as the Greek aphorism states. Have the courage to face and transform yourself.

- **Do not stand still.** Do not assume what worked yesterday will work tomorrow—and do not be so sure that what you thought worked actually did work.

- **Treasure your past,** but treasure the future more. Your best days are always ahead of you. Believe that. Live that. Be your own legacy.

I started this book by invoking Arthur Miller's *Death of a Salesman*. I will end it by saying the world does not need any more Willy Lomans. The world needs leaders who can transform themselves and the organizations they dare to lead. Do not settle for mediocrity. Be a leader—if not for yourself, then for those who would follow you and who want to believe . . . in you.

ACKNOWLEDGEMENTS

The creation of this book has been amazing in many ways. The most amazing thing is that is actually finished and that you are reading it. Few people care enough about developing their teams let alone developing themselves as leaders. I am thankful, first, to you, my reader.

My career has been filled with some fascinating people from everywhere in the world. I have also had the pleasure to learn and work with many business colleagues. They were and continue to be teachers, mentors and, most of all, special friends. I would like to acknowledge several of them here.

- Gary Hernandez, who was able to capture my voice and turned my memories, experiences, and Chicago-ese into something readable and understandable.

- Craig Nakamura, my CTO, Chief Strategist, COO, friend, thought partner and colleague without whom I could have never started my leadership journey. The fact is, everyone needs their version of "Craig" to truly transform themselves first and then the troops. He role-modeled and taught me the true difference between being a leader and a manager. He was also my "Dr. No" who could give the right message at the right time.

- Ed Daly, a leader who showed me how creativity with humbleness can be blended together to enable superior results through relationships.

- Ian Griffin, who said, "George, you should and can write a book." He shared his ability to imagine the possibilites.

- Ron Ricci, Cisco's chief evangelist who showed me how to use communications to shape the vision, strategy, culture and priorities of a company. He encouraged me to have a point of view and to share it with everyone.

- Kate Peters, or Ms. Intention, whose personal power and will to succeed propelled me through this book writing journey. She taught me the power of aligning intention with message to deliver the end result.

- Larry Liberty, my friend, colleague and executive coach, who clearly lives a life that enables his definition of a leader: "making yourself and everyone around you better."

- Jerry Ippoliti, my head coach at NIU was a role model whose energy passion filled pre-game sermons and his most memorable line, "Ok gentlemen, let's go kick some ass! Win or tie, I am right there with you. Losing is NOT an option for this team!"

- Robert E. King, my first inspirational leader, who as a CEO, was a role-model who taught me the qualities of passion, energy, drive, transparency and compassion.

- John Chambers, who provided many key lessons and observations of what to do and not to do as a CEO of a $40-billion+ public company. He was a role model who taught; intense listening, high stakes communication, how a CEO thinks, and how every message needs to resonate all the way down to the individual contributor.

- Doug Simao, my behind the scenes magic-maker, helped with all the plans and details required to produce this book, from concept to delivery. Thanks Merlin.

- Wim Elfrink, a visionary who ALWAYS built the future based upon the future and not the past. Wim was a role model with the key skills of vision, strategy and collaboration to make it happen.

- Eva Yee, my executive assistant or, as most would say, "the real SVP at Cisco." Eva for so many years helped harness the magic of our team with the power of her personality and undying commitment to customer satisfaction with everyone she touched.

- Brad Holst, my first communication coach who provided the pungent and appropriate feedback to kick-start my communication skills to the next level. Brad is a true friend who is a role model for compassion and a passion for life that cannot be restrained. His communication coaching ability is in the top 1% of those in his profession.

- Bill O'Meara, my dad whose lessons I lived and share throughout the book. If you looked in Webster's for a definition of a "consummate salesman," you would see a picture of him. He always said, "Selling is about selling. It could even be bananas; now go out there and start making those cold calls."

- Barb O'Meara, for the countless years of enduring my management journey and leadership learning curve with all the mistakes, along with listening, reading and calling BS on any content not only in the book and but also in my life.

- To all the customers and colleagues who were interviewed, a huge thanks for enduring me in the early years of my career and for the friendship and relationships that will be remembered and last a lifetime. Special thanks to Jere Brown, Geoff Moore, Larry Liberty, Craig Nakamura, Brad Holst, Nancy Clark, Mahesh Rao, Doug Dennerline, Ed Musselwhite, Corinn Hastings, Jeff Kane, Mike Staver and Woody Sessoms, whose words of wisdom were quoted in this book.

Finally I would like to thank the thousands of people I have been blessed to work with over the years.

Made in the USA
San Bernardino, CA
30 October 2013